C

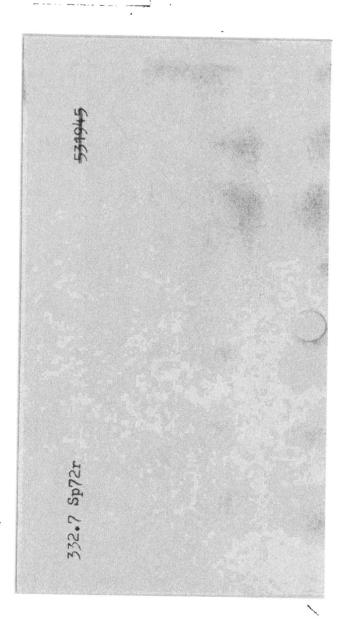

The Romance of Credit

The Romance of Credit

JESSE RAINSFORD SPRAGUE

D. APPLETON-CENTURY COMPANY
Incorporated
NEW YORK AND LONDON
1943

Foreword

It is only in rather recent years that any great number of men in our country have been engaged professionally in commercial credit work. Up to the eighteen-nineties, and even to the turn of the century, the owner of a wholesale or manufacturing enterprise was usually his own credit dispenser. But in time, as business came to be done in larger volume, the owner found it necessary to delegate portions of his work. The profession of sales manager, merchandise manager, advertising manager, came into being. Yet ordinarily, even after the business was departmentized in other respects, the owner himself continued to decide which customers should have credit and which should not. Only when the business expanded to such proportions that the owner could merely exercise general supervision, did the credit-manager profession come into being. To-day there are somewhat more than thirty thousand men employed by wholesale and manufacturing firms to devote their whole time to credit work.

The author of this book was for many years a business owner, as well as a dispenser of credit. It has been his intent to show alternately, in the various chapters, the problems of men who seek credit and those who dispense it. Some attention is also given to credit termites and camp followers. It is the author's hope that the incidents here set down, and the comments thereon, may be of some assistance to young men who are entering the credit profession, and even, perhaps, to some of the veterans.

J. R. S.

Contents

· CHAPTER I ·

Credit Built an Empire

THE WORD *credit* comes to us from ancient Rome. *Credere* is the infinitive form of the Latin word that signifies "to believe." The first person singular of the same word is *credo:* "I believe."

When, therefore, we extend credit to a person—lend him money or entrust him with goods on his promise to pay later—the transaction means that we *believe* in him. We believe he is honest. We also believe he has the ability so to conduct his affairs that he will be able to meet the obligation when the date for payment arrives.

When a credit-reporting agency lists a business firm's credit as "high," it means that the firm is considered reliable both morally and financially; producers may ship goods to the firm on time, with the assurance that the firm will make satisfactory settlement.

Except for the employment of commercial credit, it is quite possible that the United States as we know it to-day would not exist. It might now be a Spanish, or a French, country instead of an Anglo-Saxon country. When the first permanent English settlement was made at Jamestown in 1607, Spain was dominant along the southern coast, all the way from Mexico to Florida. There was a permanent Spanish population in North America of nearly two hundred thousand.

To the north, the French were established in Canada. Samuel de Champlain had explored the coast from the mouth of the St. Lawrence River down as far as Massachusetts Bay, in search of a favorable spot to plant a permanent French Colony. Had he decided to locate his colony in New England instead of Novia Scotia, there could have been no English settlement at Plymouth, and no opportunity for later generations of Americans to boast of their Pilgrim ancestry.

As matters stood, therefore, at the beginning of the seventeenth century, there was a fifteen-hundred-mile stretch of land along the coast not yet occupied by Europeans. Had the English delayed their attempts at settlements for even a few years, it is more than conceivable that Spaniards or Frenchmen would have moved in. At that time both France and Spain were richer and more populous than England; either one would have been strong enough to prevent English encroachment.

Most French and Spanish colonizing ventures were backed by the government, but that was not the case with Jamestown and Plymouth. Each was the result of a purely commercial investment, entered into for profit. Individual English business men advanced money in the belief that the colonists would earn enough to pay back the money with ample interest.

In terms of present-day currency, practically a million dollars was subscribed to finance the Jamestown project. But barely two-thirds of that sum was actually paid in. Many subscribers paid down only a part of the sum for which they subscribed, counting on quick profits to meet later instalments. They hoped for discoveries of gold and silver, similar to the discoveries of the Spaniards in Mexico and South America. In this respect the English investors were like so many Americans during our real-estate boom of the nineteen-twenties who bought city properties with a 10 per cent down payment and expected to sell at a large profit before another payment should fall due. The Jamestown investment was similar in another way to many real-estate investments of our nineteen-twenties. The investors lost their money. The Colony struggled along as a losing venture and, in 1624, became a Royal Province.

Investors in the Plymouth project fared a little better. The *Mayflower* men were small farmers, laborers, and artisans who for twelve years had supported themselves in Holland under peculiarly difficult circumstances. They were forbidden by the Dutch craftsmen's guilds to do well-paid work; yet they managed to get along. They had proved themselves to be hardy, vigorous, not easily discouraged. These things were taken into account when they applied in England for a loan to finance their American colony. English moneyed men believed it an opportunity to make a safe investment. In the phrase used by present-day credit executives the Pilgrims were considered "good for all reasonable requirements."

Yet it was a long time before the Pilgrims were able to settle with their creditors. The original loan was made for seven years; at the end of that time there was still owing what would in modern currency amount to nearly $50,000. This was not finally cleared up until twenty-five years after the landing at Plymouth.

Viewed as credit problems, Jamestown and Plymouth were radically different. Jamestown was a purely speculative venture in which the lenders went into a risky enterprise on the possibility of enormous returns through the discovery of precious minerals. They were like individuals in our western communities who "grubstake" a prospector on the chance the prospector may make a lucky strike. Wishful thinking, rather than solid security, is what prompts the outlay.

Lenders to the Plymouth enterprise, on the other hand, were on fairly safe ground. The Pilgrims were practical men, inured to hard living. They did not look for quick riches. They planned a permanent home and expected to pay for it by hard work. The money that the English financiers advanced to the Pilgrims was in every respect a Character Loan.

Little credit business was transacted in the early days of the Colonies. Money was scarce. There was no paper currency, and it was well toward a hundred years before enough silver and gold coin was in the country to supply ordinary demands of business. Goods passed hands by a system of barter. Countrymen brought corn, cheese, beaver skins to the general merchandise store and exchanged them for crockery, dress goods, or glassware imported from England, or molasses and sugar imported from the West Indies.

It was much the same procedure as exists in

many American rural sections to this day. Only recently I was commissioned to write a magazine article describing the business of a very successful country storekeeper, Mr. George M. Davis of Rock Glen, New York. Though Rock Glen is scarcely more than a wide place in the road, with fewer than a dozen dwellings, Mr. Davis' sales amount to $250,000 a year. Customers come to him from forty miles roundabout. A considerable portion of Mr. Davis' business is done without any exchange of money, just as in the early days of Virginia and Massachusetts. Farmers bring in their commodities and swap them for goods in Mr. Davis' general stock —sugar, ladies' ready-to-wear dresses, wall-paper, shoes, plow-points.

The only difference between Mr. Davis and the Colonial merchant of three hundred years ago is that Mr. Davis pays his manufacturers and wholesalers in cash. He sells across his own counters the commodities that he gets from his farmer customers. But the early Colonial merchant didn't have cash. He paid *his* bills with the farm products he swapped for. When he received a consignment of manufactured goods from England, or tropical products from the West Indies, he shipped back wheat, rye, muskrat skins, and potatoes to settle the bill.

As the population of the Colonies increased and

people pushed inland, away from the coast settlements, the primitive barter system had necessarily to be modified. It was impossible for a man who had settled in the Berkshires to carry his farm products to Massachusetts Bay for swapping purposes, or a Valley of Virginia man to carry his produce to Jamestown. Small traders followed the pioneers to the new western settlements and opened general stores. These storekeepers were not strong enough financially to import manufactured goods from abroad; they bought goods from larger merchants in coast towns who did import. These coast merchants became America's first wholesalers. The wholesaler-retailer-consumer system came naturally into existence.

With this change some sort of credit became a necessity. The small interior storekeeper had somewhat to be financed by his wholesaler. There were, of course, no credit agencies to pass on the responsibility, or otherwise, of interior storekeepers. Sometimes a storekeeper would send in an order for goods and accompany it with a letter of recommendation from the village pastor or some leading citizen. Often a wholesaler wrote for information concerning a prospective customer to several persons in the prospect's community.

It was customary for early wholesalers to extend credit of three to six months to their storekeeper customers. Longer credit terms became increasingly necessary as population moved still farther from the coast, out into what we now call the Middle West. Transportation was slow; there was a long interval between the time the storekeeper sent in his order and the time the merchandise was laid on his doorstep. A storekeeper in western Kentucky, for example, who sent an order to some New York or Philadelphia wholesaler, could scarcely count on receiving his goods within three months.

There was another reason for long credit terms. So long as the country was nearly all agricultural, the rural storekeeper was obliged to put a large proportion of his sales on his books. He supplied his farmer customers with goods throughout the year, but got his money only in the fall when the farmers sold their crops. The storekeeper, generally not too well financed, had to depend on his wholesaler to carry him from one autumn to the next. By the beginning of the eighteen-hundreds, it seems to have been the general practice for wholesalers to grant their storekeeper customers a full year's time on purchases.

Early in the eighteen-hundreds America began to change from an agricultural country into a manufacturing country. Our manufacturing plants had progressed to the point where we were no longer dependent on Europe for any great proportion of manufactured goods. But until after the Civil War, and even into the present century, domestic trade mainly passed through the hands of wholesalers. Manufacturers did not ordinarily sell their products direct to retail dealers. They sold to wholesalers. Wholesalers, in turn, sold to retailers.

Some wholesale concerns grew to huge proportions. In the seventies and eighties of the last century the textile house of Claflin in New York City did a business of nearly $100,000,000 a year; the same volume, if sold at present-day prices, would figure almost double that sum. The Simmons Hardware Company of St. Louis sent its salesmen to every part of the country and even did a considerable export business. Ely-Walker Company, also of St. Louis, did a nation-wide trade in dry goods; Hamilton-Brown of the same city in shoes; Sprague-Warner of Chicago in groceries.

Besides these great concerns that specialized in different lines, there were hundreds of "regional" wholesalers who carried general stocks and supplied storekeepers in their immediate territories. These regional wholesalers carried on business in much the same way as the importing houses of the early Colonial period. They extended long credit. Often, in fact, there were no formal credit terms at all. The storekeeper came to the wholesale house once a year, usually in September, and ordered merchandise enough to carry on for the next twelve months. There was a mutual understanding that the storekeeper would pay the bill a little at a time, as he was able. In many cases the storekeeper's account was never balanced; it ran on from year to year.

The great days of wholesaling began to fade out at about the end of the eighteen-nineties. With the new century there was a demand for greater efficiency in the distribution of merchandise. It was the beginning of the muckraking era. A whole coterie of writer-economists sprang up who attacked the existing system and branded the wholesaler as a useless burden on society. Frequently, some rather sensational statements were made as to the large profits exacted by wholesalers. These profits, the writers demanded, should be eliminated and the savings passed on to the public through lower prices. Manufacturers should go over the wholesalers' heads and sell direct to retail storekeepers.

Those articles appearing in various journals probably convinced many retailers that they owed it to themselves and to their public to buy "direct." About the same time another development helped along the trend toward direct buying. The first years of the present century marked the beginning of really efficient national advertising. Before that, one might say, manufacturers' publicity was a bit lacking in resourcefulness. An advertisement was apt to consist of a picture of the factory with perhaps a photograph of the factory president in one corner; or general claims as to the merit of a product, like, "Garland Stoves and Ranges are Best"; "A Rogers Group in Every Home"; "Wear Plymouth Rock Celebrated Three Dollar Pants."

Advertisements became more sophisticated, but advertisers soon learned that printed publicity alone could not do the whole job. It was necessary to back up printed publicity by more intensive salesmanship. But intensive salesmanship was not possible for a manufacturer who depended on wholesale houses to distribute his product. A wholesaler who handled the products of a great many manufacturers had to give equal service to all. He could not afford to push any one manufacturer's product intensively.

That is the reason why so many manufacturers abandoned the wholesaler during the early years of this century and began selling direct to the retailer. The immediate result was a shortening of credits. A manufacturer who sold a single specialty could not afford to give a retail merchant the same easy terms as the old-time wholesale house that sold the merchant his entire stock. In a comparatively few years credit terms in many lines shrank from a comfortable twelve months to thirty days, or even less. In some lines there were no credit terms at all. Automobile manufacturers, for example, demanded cash in advance from dealers. The Ford Motor Company inaugurated the "quota" system that went even further than cash in advance. Before 1914 the Ford Company was dictating to every Ford dealer the number of cars he must buy. In case a dealer refused to buy his "quota," the company put him out of business.

In more recent years commercial credit terms have fluctuated according to economic conditions. During the First World War and for a year or two afterward, when merchandise was scarce and it was believed there would be a scarcity for some time to come, credit was doled out with a niggardly hand. Only a merchant who enjoyed an extra high rating in Dun's and Bradstreet's could send in an order for goods or materials and be reasonably sure his order would be filled. Orders from less highly rated merchants were placed on an indefinite waiting list.

That phase ended in 1920. Production caught up with demand sooner than was anticipated. Goods piled up in manufacturers' warehouses. The public first learned of changed conditions in May when John Wanamaker, the New York and Philadelphia department-store owner, announced in newspaper advertisements his belief that the shortage was over and prices were too high. He offered a 20 per cent discount on all purchases in his two immense stores. Other merchants followed with more radical reductions; by December of that year goods all over the country were being offered at half price or less.

Hard times continued for approximately three years. By then surplus stocks were fairly worked off, and almost overnight depression turned into the greatest boom in the country's history. Optimism was in the air. Credit was offered lavishly by manufacturers and bankers on the assumption that prosperity had come for good. Individual business men in all parts of the country have told me of being accosted by some local banker with the remark, "Couldn't you use some extra money to advantage in your business? If so, come on down to the bank." Credit was hawked about as though it were a brand of merchandise.

The long depression that followed the débâcle of 1929 is too recent to warrant detailed description here. One curious result of the depression from a credit standpoint was a reversion to the selling practices of the eighteen-hundreds. With sharply reduced volume some manufacturers found it too expensive to send salesmen to solicit business from storekeepers in widely scattered towns and villages. It was expensive, too, to watch credits and handle collections on the small amounts purchased; particularly so as a good many storekeepers were financially shaky and not in position to pay their bills promptly.

In some cases a manufacturer would continue to sell direct to large-city merchants, but arrange with regional wholesalers to sell his product in small places. In other cases manufacturers abandoned direct selling altogether and distributed through the wholesale trade.

There is no doubt but that wholesaler distribution tends toward fewer retailer failures. When a storekeeper owes money to manufacturers who are a long way off, and who know him only from figures printed in the books of credit reporting agencies, it is a strictly business matter. In a spell of hard times the retailer can not expect the same neighborly treatment that he gets from his near-by wholesaler who not only knows him personally, but knows he is doing his best to pay his bills as they fall due.

Credit isn't an ordinary commodity, like groceries or dry-goods. It is an intangible thing, born of one man's confidence in another man's integrity. When the Pilgrims borrowed money to finance their Colony they didn't have anything to put up as security. All the security the creditors had was character. But the creditors got their money back, with interest.

·CHAPTER II·

Good and Bad Financing

YEARS AGO, when the elder J. Pierpont Morgan stated to a committee of United States senators that he made loans on the basis of character, there were consequences of a not altogether beneficial nature. The financier's remark made good newspaper copy. Editorial and Sunday supplement writers seized on the idea and have since produced uncounted thousands of words designed to prove that if a man's character be above reproach he needs no other asset in order to secure whatever capital he requires. But unfortunately many of these writers seem to confuse the word *character* with *honesty*. Their articles often convey the idea that if a man is simply honest, his credit standing is assured.

Which is decidedly not the case. Honesty is not a rare quality. Ninety-nine persons out of one hundred are basically honest. Honesty is only one element of a man's character that the dispenser of credit considers. Had Mr. Morgan extended his statement he would doubtless have said that honesty must be supplemented by business ability and judgment; that the would-be borrower must prove that the business for which he wishes to borrow has a more than even chance of success.

I am sure Mr. Morgan, had he spoken his full mind, would have said further that to be a first-class credit risk a man must consider permanent stability above immediate large profits. He himself, it was said, never charged a borrower more than 6 per cent interest. Mr. John K. Winkler, in his book, *Morgan the Magnificent,* quotes the financier as alluding disparagingly to certain opportunist Wall Street money-lenders as "The Ten Per Cent Crowd."

Some years ago I was commissioned by the Lehigh Portland Cement Company to write a book on the cement industry. When completed, the book was sent as a gift to several thousand firms throughout the country. For a long time the Lehigh Company had operated on the policy of selling its product exclusively to retail building-material dealers.

The Company had passed up millions of dollars' worth of sales, I was told, by rigidly adhering to this rule.

It often happened in some town that a building contractor would secure an important contract, such as a new high school, or court-house, and naturally would wish to buy his materials as cheaply as possible. In such a case he might approach several large cement producers and ask to purchase his supplies direct from them and so save the retail dealer's profit. The Lehigh Company always refused to do business with him. If the contractor wished to use Lehigh cement he would have to buy it from some retail building-material dealer in his town.

The contractor might argue that the quantity of cement he wished to buy would amount to more than any local retailer purchased in a year. Lehigh's answer was always the same: "We cannot sell you direct because that would not be fair to the dealers in your town. True, the amount of cement you wish to purchase for your present building job is more than a retailer buys in a year; but yours is a one-time purchase; you may not be in the market again for a long time. The retailer, on the other hand, is a regular customer of ours. For our own interest as well as his, we must protect him."

Occasionally the contractor might persuade some

cement producer to sell him direct, in which case Lehigh lost the sale. Yet Lehigh officials believed their policy was sound. They were building a solid future for their concern.

In merchandising circles there is an old saying that there is no profit in a single sale; that profit comes only through a succession of sales continued over a long period. The same principle applies to banking. Few bankers care to do business with a man who appears to lack the qualities that make for permanent success, even though at the moment the man may be good for the loan he requests. If loans are granted when the man is prosperous it would be embarrassing, to say the least, to refuse accommodation to the man in case of adversity. Always, a banker has in mind these questions: Is this man likely to be permanently successful? Will he be a safe risk ten years from now?

Some bankers consider it a bad sign for a man or corporation to be overenterprising. Some time ago the National Bank of Commerce in New York published a booklet disparaging a new enterprise that was being advertised by a "well-known concern." For a reasonable fee this concern would give merchants and manufacturers daily reports of beneficiaries of wills in the five metropolitan boroughs. Names and addresses of persons who had been left cash in amounts from $25,000 upward would be furnished, along with the exact amount each person received.

The writer of the National Bank of Commerce booklet condemned the advertised service on the grounds that it overstepped the bounds of legitimate business enterprise. Nor was his condemnation confined to the violation of ethics contained in the ghoulish scheme. He intimated that subscribers to the service might eventually find their businesses seriously hurt on account of resentment in the minds of persons who were brazenly solicited to spend the money received from recently deceased loved ones. Reading between the lines it is not difficult to imagine that neither the "well-known concern" nor its subscribers would be cordially welcomed by the bank as borrowing customers.

Recently I had occasion to interview the president of another large New York bank, and in the course of conversation I mentioned meeting, on a trip through the Pacific Northwest, a young salesman who had quit the big eastern manufacturing corporation he formerly represented to go with a smaller concern. He quit the corporation, he said, because of its high-powered tactics. Salesmen were ordered to sell a certain volume, no matter what condition the territory might be in. Regional salesmanagers constantly wrote threatening letters to keep salesmen on their toes. Merchandise was pushed on dealers without regard to their opportunities for disposing of it. The young salesman said his present concern didn't operate that way. His job was much pleasanter.

With this in mind I asked the New York banker: "Do you, in scanning a corporation's statement with view of making a loan, take into account the corporation's methods of securing business? If the corporation uses extreme high-pressure tactics, such as my salesman friend out in Idaho described, would that influence your decision in extending or refusing credit?"

The banker replied that in such a case he would go even further than to refuse credit. He said he could mention a very prominent corporation from which his bank had declined to accept an account. Yet the corporation's financial position at the time was absolutely sound. Its debts were not too much for its capital. Its volume of sales had shown an increase from year to year. It was paying substantial dividends.

But there was a fly in the ointment, the banker said. The corporation had built its volume on extreme high-pressure salesmanship. Each year it had decreed a volume far in excess of the previous year. It had forced its salesmen to make nuisances of themselves.

The banker predicted that some day the corporation would pay for these things. Already there was a healthy competitor doing business along lines of reasonable conservatism and making fair progress. The older corporation was in no position to meet competition. It had no organization worthy of the name. Secretly, the people who had done its high-powered work would resent the things they were compelled to do. If events should begin to turn against it, the corporation's decline might be sensational.

Those were the reasons, the banker said, for his declining to accept the corporation's proffered account. He didn't believe the corporation would permanently be a safe risk for loans it might ask for. That being the case, he thought it best to stay out of the corporation's affairs altogether.

It is worth noting that concerns that have been in existence a long time have always looked after their credit standing very keenly. With them the financing of operations was more important than sales volume or immediate profits. The Albany Iron and Hardware Company, of Albany, New York, has a record of success extending well over one hundred years. In the concern's archives there is a copy of a letter, written in the fall of 1836 by the head of the concern and addressed to a manufacturer in Sheffield, England, where he was in the habit of buying fine cutlery and small tools. It was during the presidency of Andrew Jackson, when the United States was in a most prosperous condition, and to many Americans the prosperity appeared to be permanent. But the old gentleman in Albany must have had the gift of foresight as well as financial acumen, because he confided to the Sheffield manufacturer that many Americans were spending beyond their means; he feared business was too brisk to continue at the prevailing rate, and if a stringency should occur, he might not be able to pay his invoices as promptly as in the past. "I will therefore ask you," the old gentleman's letter concluded, "to ship only half the merchandise that I ordered in my recent communication."

There is no record to show if the Sheffield Manufacturer granted the old gentleman's request, though it may be assumed he did, for the Albany Iron and Hardware Company weathered the business débâcle of 1837 without apparent difficulty.

There is a business story of a much later date that turned out less fortunately because the head of a prominent business was more concerned with immediate profits than with maintaining his credit standing. Though I do not feel free to give the name of the concern, I will state that I myself did considerable business with it when I operated retail stores. The facts are essentially as follows:

It was an eastern manufacturing corporation that over a period of forty years had built up an enormous sale on a line of specialties that it distributed through wholesale houses from coast to coast. The line was so well and favorably known that selling was almost automatic. Wholesalers made money on the line. The corporation allowed them a 15 per cent profit.

Along in the nineteen-twenties, when business everywhere was going at high speed, the head of the corporation, whom I will call Mr. Blank, considered eliminating the wholesalers and selling direct to the retail trade. Before coming definitely to a decision he sent a crew of salesmen to call on retailers in a mid-western area, and the experiment resulted in what he believed to be confirmation of his plan. In one month's trial of direct selling the figures showed a sales expense of slightly less than 10 per cent. On the strength of this Mr. Blank changed the sales policy of his company.

In retrospect it is easy to point out that the experiment was scarcely conducted on a broad enough scale; that while direct selling might be done at a cost of less than 10 per cent in the thickly populated area that the crew of salesmen covered, it might be far more expensive in some western states where towns are much farther apart and traveling expenses greater. But it was a time of general optimism, just as in the Andrew Jackson era, and people were inclined to wishful thinking. There was another matter that apparently was not considered. Wholesalers who had handled the line and made money on it naturally would resent the manufacturer's going over their heads. They would not forego their accustomed profits without a struggle.

The manufacturer's line was the most popular line on the market and of really good quality, yet wholesalers had to have something to take its place; most of them found similar goods that they could recommend and sell to their retailer-customers. On the shelves of thousands of small retail shops the manufacturer's products disappeared and were superseded by competing brands, guaranteed by regional wholesalers from whom the retailers bought general merchandise supplies.

The manufacturer lost business from another cause. Many retailers throughout the country had financial ratings of such a fragile character that it was unwise to sell them without close and constant supervision. Naturally, the manufacturer, trying to do a country-wide business from its eastern headquarters, had to pass up these uncertain risks. But the wholesalers who operated in strictly local territories could take more chances because they were in almost daily contact with such dealers. Often a wholesaler would take over a distressed merchant and supervise the business until the merchant's affairs were in a healthy condition.

The eastern manufacturer could afford to lose some business; when Mr. Blank changed its selling policy the corporation had book assets of some $7,-000,000, including plant, stock on hand, and accounts receivable. But there were certain flaws in Mr. Blank's reckoning. He had reduced his cash surplus by making extensive additions to his plant. Then, too, when the corporation sold its products to wholesalers it received its money promptly—usually within two weeks; for wholesalers almost invariably discounted their bills. But all this was changed when the corporation began selling to retail dealers. Few of these discounted, and many took an unreasonably long time to settle. Instead of the corporation getting its money in two weeks, the average was more than two months. It was doing about $10,000 worth of business a day during the latter part of the nineteen-twenties. This meant that $500,000 of its capital was tied up in book accounts.

Mr. Blank made another financial mistake. He could easily have got additional capital; he chose instead to borrow $1,000,000 from New York banks. In addition, he issued notes for another $1,000,000 that he disposed of to Wall Street brokers. There was no reason why he should have split up his obligations in this manner, except the fact that he could get money on his notes at half of one per cent less than his banks charged him.

That was his vital mistake. When the panic of 1929 occurred his sales fell off; receipts were not sufficient to pay the notes that he had sold to Wall Street brokers and that were falling due. When he went to his banks and asked for money to wipe out these obligations, he was quite naturally informed that while the banks would be glad to renew loans they themselves had made, they did not feel like making new loans for the purpose of paying debts to other people.

In the meantime prices on merchandise of every sort had gone down. The corporation had a tremendous stock of finished goods on hand; the shrinkage in value cut considerably into the $7,000,000 statement Mr. Blank made at the time he borrowed from his banks and from Wall Street brokers. This led to another unwise move. Mr. Blank recruited an army of high-powered salesman and sent them through the country with orders to get rid of merchandise by every means possible. Extra-long credits were granted to merchants who would buy in quantities; where long credits were no inducement, the salesmen were empowered to place goods on consignment. This campaign cost a great deal of money. It is said that the corporation's selling costs ran as high as 50 per cent.

Finally a bankers' committee took charge of the corporation's affairs. The committee's first move was to reduce prices on the stock of finished goods, and this cut down the corporation's original valuation by a million dollars. But this was only a beginning. As soon as the reduced prices were announced to the trade, merchandise that had been put out on consignment began coming back in huge quantities. A great deal of the merchandise that had actually been sold also came back. There was little chance for argument in such cases. The high-pressure salesmen had made so many fictitious promises that there was no alternative other than to submit to every claim.

A receivership followed the bankers' committee. During these two régimes the shrinkage in values and the losses in operation brought the corporation's assets down to $4,000,000, and the money borrowed in New York was still unpaid. When the business was finally disposed of at forced sale, it did not bring enough money to pay the creditors in full.

· CHAPTER III ·

The Danger Point

WHEN THE trade press announces some firm's bankruptcy and attempts to analyze the cause, any one of half a dozen phrases are liable to be used: Insufficient Capital; Lack of Experience; Inattention to Business; Extravagance of Owners, etc. But seldom is a phrase used to describe a situation that brings about an enormous number of bankruptcies: *Surplus Money.*

Let us see just what that means. Perhaps I can best explain by telling what happened to a man in one of the larger Virginia cities, whom I used to know quite intimately. A few years ago he was owner of a prosperous lumber business. Working up from small beginnings he had got to the point where he discounted all his purchases and had about $15,000 lying idle in the bank. Commercial agencies rated him at $100,000, his credit was unquestioned. Now his business is gone and he is working as salesman for a lumber concern in another city.

It was his surplus money that started him on the downward path. He worried because the fifteen thousand dollars wasn't earning anything. There was a small town some fifty miles away, for which people predicted a wonderful future. It had water transportation and was on a branch of a main-line railroad. The lumberman heard from what he considered an unimpeachable source that one of the big automobile companies was about to build a huge assembly-plant in the town, that would employ three thousand men. If that happened, other industries would move in and the town would become a sizable city with new stores, schools, churches, and all the rest. The lumberman thought it was too good a chance to miss. He bought a tract of land near where he believed the retail district of the coming city would be. He paid down his fifteen thousand dollars in cash and gave a series of notes for the balance, amounting to something like $48,000.

He had no idea he would ever have to meet any

of these notes; he expected to sell his property at a big advance before they fell due. But there was some hitch and the automobile assembly-plant went to another town. The property that the lumberman bought remained pasture land. He had to meet the notes out of the profits of his lumber business, and the profits weren't enough. Whenever a note fell due he paid it with money that should have gone to pay merchandise bills. He became so slow in paying for merchandise that he lost his high credit rating. Some manufacturers declined to sell him except on a C.O.D. basis. Then it was only a question of time before he was out of business altogether.

This unhappy story of my Virginia lumberman friend could truly be repeated, with variations, a thousand times and from every part of the country. When I was myself in retail business we had a merchant in town who was just about the most conservative man I have ever known. Hardy was a man in his late forties, a bachelor, who had a men's furnishing store at the upper end of Main Street near the shoe factory. He slept in the back of his store and took his meals at Mrs. Reed's boarding-house around the corner at a cost of something like four-fifty a week.

Hardy's store expenses also were down to a minimum. He got along without a clerk and did his own sweeping and window washing. On Saturday afternoons when the shoe factory paid off and the workmen came along with wages in their pockets, he hung work shirts and overalls all over the front of his store and personally solicited trade. He wouldn't join the chamber of commerce on account of the $15 a year dues, and whenever a committee went along Main Street to solicit money for the spring carnival or the Baseball Association he always said, "I guess you'll have to pass me up this time; my trade is awfully slow just now."

By similar economies he managed over the years to save up $10,000. That was the danger point for Hardy. What he did with his money may seem unbelievable, but it really happened. A promoter came along who was organizing a company in a near-by city to manufacture balloons. He convinced Hardy that the balloon industry had wonderful possibilities. Hardy bought stock in the promoter's company, which turned out a dud. He lost his $10,000.

It will be necessary to dip into psychology a bit to figure out why some men who are ultra-conservative in their own business will take long chances when they have surplus money to invest. A reasonable explanation is that every business appears more attractive when looked at from the outside than from the inside. You know all the snags and drawbacks of your own business. You know there isn't any such thing as easy money in it. You don't make a dollar unless you work for it.

But you see some man in another line of business who doesn't appear to have any worries at all. Of course, his cheerful countenance may conceal an aching heart, but you can't know that. You suspect his business may have some hidden advantage unknown to yours. Anyhow, the less you know about the other man's business the more attractive it appears. And so, when you have surplus money you are inclined to invest it in some enterprise as different from your own business as possible.

It sometimes happens that experienced business men invest money in some enterprise that they think they understand, but make the mistake of overlooking some important detail. Up to a few years ago in Paris, France, the Duval restaurants were among the most popular eating places of that metropolis. There were thirty of them, scattered about the city, catering to all classes; those on the Grand Boulevards were quite de luxe, others in working-class sections were plain; but the food was always good. The founder, Monsieur Duval, started his career as a journeyman cook, and his interest in the art did not slacken even after he became a very wealthy man. Rain or shine he visited each one of his thirty restaurants every day.

I was in Paris, after an absence of a couple of years, just before the Second World War started, and noticed there were no Duval restaurants. Some locations had been taken over by other lines of business, and some had their fronts boarded up with "For Rent" signs tacked on. I noticed one place where an enterprising beverage manufacturer had tacked an advertising sign on the shutters: "This place failed because of the owner's indigestion. Drink SUZE. It is the friend of the stomach."

A French business man friend told me what it was that put the Duval restaurants out of business. Monsieur Duval reached the age of eighty and wished to retire. His only son refused to be a restaurateur; his ambition was to become a champion tennis player. At this juncture Monsieur Duval had an unexpected opportunity to dispose of his business. There was in France a very rich and successful wholesale grocery corporation that operated branches in leading cities throughout the country. This corporation, Felix Potin, bought the Duval business.

The wholesale grocery executives had every reason to believe they made a profitable move. They had a large cash surplus, so they were not cramping themselves financially. They were not going into an entirely unfamiliar business. For years they had specialized in selling to the restaurant trade, not only in Paris, but all over France. Monsieur Duval had been one of their best customers. In buying his thirty restaurants they figured they would make a double profit—the regular profit on goods they furnished the restaurants, and the profits that the restaurants earned as well.

But things did not turn out that way. The French people are connoisseurs in the matter of food; rightly or wrongly there were complaints that the standard of cookery was not quite as high as formerly under Monsieur Duval's expert supervision. Business of the restaurants fell off.

Then a still more formidable obstacle turned up. Independent owners of Paris restaurants quit buying supplies from the Potin wholesale house. Potin was no longer a friend, but a competitor. The same thing happened in other places where Potin maintained branch establishments. Provincial restaurateurs reasoned that if Potin chose to enter the restaurant business in Paris, it might do so in their communities.

Affairs got to the point where the Potin executives had to choose between losing their restaurateur customers, or getting out of the restaurant business. They chose the latter, and closed up the thirty restaurants they had bought. The money they invested in them was a dead loss.

Recently on a business trip across the United States I called on a bank president in a Texas city. The banker was at his desk in the railed-off space at the front of the banking room, talking with a customer. Apparently the customer didn't like some advice the banker was giving him. Two or three times he shook his head impatiently and directly got up to go. Then I heard the banker say, "Anyhow, Mr. Smith, I hope you won't do anything with this money that may jeopardize your regular business."

Later on the banker told me what the conversation was about. Mr. Smith owns a woodworking plant where he makes crates and boxes for wholesale houses and manufacturers. He started on small capital a dozen or so years ago, and has his building and equipment all paid for. At the beginning of the present year he was in much the same position as my lumberman friend in Virginia; he had an accumulation of about $15,000 that he didn't need in his woodworking business.

He had been talking with the banker about a scheme he had for putting this money to work. He would put up a new building next to his box factory and start making a line of inexpensive bookshelves, desks, and tables to sell to furniture dealers throughout the state. He said he could produce these things cheaper than any one else because his expenses would be so low. Some of the mechanical work could be done right in his box factory. He would personally supervise both plants.

"It isn't as though I were going into a new line of business," he told the banker. "I'm just adding a department to my regular business."

The banker disagreed with that. "I'm afraid you're fooling yourself, Mr. Smith," he said. "It's an entirely new industry you're figuring on. You haven't any connections with the retail furniture trade. You'd have to start from scratch and work up a new set of customers. That takes time. You'd run the risk of using up your $15,000 before you got your furniture plant on a paying basis."

"If I found it didn't pay," Mr. Smith argued, "I could drop it."

The banker disagreed again. "Yes, I know you could drop it, Mr. Smith," he said. "But the question is, *would* you drop it? Because there is always the temptation to say to yourself, 'I'm not going to give up yet. It's bound to turn the corner pretty soon.' "

Mr. Smith started to interrupt, but the banker kept on: "So you start throwing good money after bad. You take money that you make in your box factory to bolster up your furniture factory. You know what that means as well as I do if you keep it up long enough."

Mr. Smith didn't make any reply to that. He looked at the banker a moment, then went out of the bank.

I asked the banker if he believed Mr. Smith would heed his warning. He wasn't sure. "My friend Smith is likely to be pretty obstinate about this thing. The spare money he's got is burning a hole in his pocket. He's cooked up a scheme that is highly impractical. But when a man starts to do wishful thinking there isn't much you can do to stop him."

It is to be hoped the box manufacturer heeded the banker's warning. Because wishful thinking is a dangerous pastime that has wrecked the fortune of many a business man. I happen to know one extreme case. In a rural New York community that I am familiar with, there was a farmer whose place was a couple of miles from the village. When Henry reached middle age he had his farm all paid for and could afford to keep a hired man the year around. Whether or not it was freedom from financial worry and having idle time on his hands, no one seemed to know, but Henry developed into something of a sport. He went to the village every day and smoked cigars. He also began to do considerable wishful thinking. "One of these days," he was always saying, "I bet I'm going to go into some business that's easier to make money in than plowing and pitching hay."

One autumn a few years ago Henry went over to the county seat when the annual fair and horse races were on, and made the acquaintance of a genial fellow who operated a merry-go-round. When the merry-go-round man moved his machine to the next county fair, Henry went with him. Apparently the business appealed to Henry as the answer to his wishful thinking, because when the county fair season was over, Henry mortgaged his farm for money to buy a half interest in the merry-go-round, and the two friends went off on a tour of the southern states with it.

Henry is back home now, but he hasn't any farm. He peddles vegetables from door to door around the village.

There is one good rule to follow if you get to the point where you are on easy street and are looking around for outside investment: whatever you invest in, pay cash down. Don't take on obligations that may plague you later on. To be sure, you might lose the cash that you put into the outside investment, but that would be the end of it. There would be no temptation to keep throwing good money after bad.

There are all sorts of temptations to go wrong when you have debts all paid and money in the bank. You have, for example, a competitor who is a confirmed price-cutter. Whenever a good piece of business is in sight, he slashes his figures down to cost or less—anything to get the order. He may do this so often that it finally gets on your nerves and you decide to buy him out and get rid of his competition.

That is precisely what a very important manufacturing concern did a few years ago. I will not mention the concern's name, but merely state it is one that is well known from coast to coast. The concern not only used its cash reserves but borrowed money from banks to buy the plant of a price-cutting competitor. Recently an official of the concern told me the plant has been a headache ever since. The plant had got its business mainly by making price-concessions to dealers; when the plant changed hands, and dealers could no longer get their price-concessions, they shopped around for other sources of supply. The concern hasn't yet got out of debt to the banks it borrowed money from. The official is firmly of the opinion that the best way to get rid of a price-cutting competitor is to let him keep on doing business below cost until he bankrupts himself. "That will happen if you give him time enough," the official said.

There is a merchant whose store is in a residential section of a city of a quarter million population in the Middle West. The merchant has done well and accumulated a considerable surplus. He thought of two ways for investing his money. One plan was to buy from his landlord the building he occupied. The other plan, which he liked better, was to quit the suburban location altogether and open a bigger store in the main business district of the city.

He talked over his plans with a friend who is president of a Chicago wholesale house. The wholesaler advised him to buy his building and stay where he was. Downtown rents were high. The merchant would have to pay at least $700 a month for the sort of store he needed. Other expenses would be in proportion. He would have to do fully three times the business he was doing in his residential location barely to make expenses in the high-pressure district.

The merchant admitted all that might be true, but he was inclined to take a chance. He believed he knew how to run a store as well as any one. Others were making a go of it in the high-rent district, so why shouldn't he?

"You'd have to run your store differently in the downtown district," the wholesaler told him. "You're successful where you are because you're a good salesman and people like to trade with you. But downtown you wouldn't have time to do much personal selling or to be sociable with people. You'd have to organize a force of assistants to do those things. You'd succeed or fail according to how good an organizer you are."

The wholesaler proposed a scheme that the merchant agreed to. The wholesaler would instruct a credit agency to send one of its best men to interview the merchant at his store and then make a confidential report. "I'll merely tell the credit agency," the wholesaler said, "that you think of moving down to the high-rent district and that I want to know, in case you do, if it will be safe for me to extend you a liberal amount of credit."

In a few days the credit agency reporter called at the merchant's store, where he spent part of a day going through the merchant's books, asking questions and observing how the business was run. Later on the credit man's report was sent to the Chicago wholesaler.

The report sized the merchant up from all angles. It complimented him on the orderliness of his store. It stated he was very popular with customers. But in other ways the report was less flattering. It said the merchant had a "one-man business"; that he seemed to be of salesman type rather than of organizing type; that many customers refused to be waited on by his clerks and insisted on the merchant's waiting on them personally, and that the merchant apparently encouraged it.

At the end the report said: "These things may be a favorable sign in a suburban store, but would be a serious drawback in a congested business center where expenses are too high to be met by one person's activities." And the very last sentence was: "Should the merchant make the move he contemplates, it is recommended that wholesalers who do business with him should watch his account closely."

The merchant decided to let well enough alone. He bought his store building and settled down there for good. The Chicago wholesaler who told me the story says the merchant passed the danger point of his business with flying colors.

· CHAPTER IV ·

Bank Credit

UNION SQUARE, in New York City, is a favorite gathering place for soap-box orators who are dissatisfied with existing economic conditions. On one occasion I heard an orator with a loud voice, but no collar or necktie, discuss capitalism. He explained how simple it is, under a capitalistic régime, to become a rich business man.

Five large banks face Union Square. The orator pointed to each one in turn: "All you've got to do is to go to one of them banks and borrow some capital. You take your capital and start a big store or factory. Then you exploit the workers and make your millions."

It was all very encouraging; but one could not

help feeling that the orator failed to go into sufficient detail. He did not explain what one must do to persuade a banker to advance money with which to start the store or factory.

How, really, does a banker choose the people he is willing to put on his books for loans? Of one thing we may be certain. A banker is seldom influenced by ingenious schemes devised by would-be borrowers. I have heard various schemes advanced, and one of the most popular goes something like this:

You become acquainted with the president or cashier of a bank—preferably on the Country Club golf links—and after a time you go to the bank and negotiate a loan of $1,000, either on the indorsement of some moneyed relative or by putting up certain collateral. The note you give runs sixty days. You do not draw out your $1,000, but leave it to your credit. A few days before the note falls due you drop into the bank and give a check to wipe out your indebtedness. The banker notices how prompt you have been. And because you didn't draw out the money you borrowed, the banker assumes that you are a man of large affairs who probably intended to make some investment, but decided at last it was not worthwhile to do so. Anyhow, the banker sets you down as a first-class credit risk, and afterward will loan you money on your own signature.

Sometimes, if you are extra clever and wish to pull the wool over the banker's eyes more completely, you actually withdraw the $1,000 from his bank and deposit it in another institution for the sixty-day period. This inclines the banker to believe you have used the money in some profitable transaction. He thinks of you as a shrewd financier.

Though these schemes are doubtless as old as banking itself, certain individuals still have faith in them. Within a week previous to writing these lines, a man who is old enough to know better has said to me, "The clever way to establish bank credit is to borrow $1,000—"

The principal drawback to the plan is that, like most short cuts, it doesn't work. No bank executive with enough acumen to be intrusted with the loaning of depositors' funds will by any chance be influenced by such transparent scheming.

I trust I may be pardoned if I bring in a personal reminiscence that has to do with establishing bank credit. I was in my early twenties when I went to Newport News, Virginia, to open a retail store. I had a fair knowledge of merchandising from several years' experience as a retail salesman, but my knowledge of finance and banking was exceedingly sketchy. I had been in business but a short time when one day a prominent citizen came into my store and selected goods amounting to $50; then he pulled a printed form out of his pocket, filled in the blank spaces and handed it to me with the remark, "This will be all right, I assume?" I glanced at the paper, saw the figure $50 in one corner and the citizen's signature at the bottom; I thanked him for his business and dropped the paper in my cash drawer. That night when I counted my receipts I noticed the paper bore the wording "Sixty days from date," but did not pay much attention, believing it to be some unusual form of check that the gentleman chose to use. I learned afterward that the gentleman, while perfectly solvent, was such a liberal spender that he was chronically short of cash and had a habit of paying for purchases with notes in order to gain extra time.

Next day when I went to the First National Bank I put the document along with my currency and handed the deposit in at the receiving teller's window. The teller glanced at the paper and said, "Do you want to discount this note? If so, I'd speak to the cashier." I realized then that I had committed a *faux pas* of some sort and said hurriedly, "Oh, no, I guess I brought it along by mistake. I'll take it back to the store." The transaction gave me such an inferiority complex that for a long time afterward I disliked going to the bank, imagining the clerks must be chuckling over my naïveté.

One day, at the end of the following December, a friend dropped into my store and asked how my business was coming along. I told him I had done fairly well, though I had overbought a bit on holiday goods. I lacked about $1,000 to pay my bills and earn the 5 per cent cash discount that my wholesalers allowed on first-of-the-month payments. The friend asked why I didn't go to the First National and borrow the amount I needed. When I said I didn't believe I could get it, he remarked cynically, "There's no harm in trying. You aren't afraid of the bank, are you?"

I still had my inferiority complex on account of the note transaction; it was two or three days before I could bring myself to make the attempt. When I went in I approached the cashier and said awkwardly, "Mr. Willett, I want to borrow $1,000." Mr. Willett's response was discouraging. "You know," he said, "we don't loan money for permanent capital." I explained that I wasn't looking for permanent capital, but wanted money to discount merchandise bills. He said that was different. Then he asked when I figured on paying the money in case he loaned it to me. I said I believed I could settle at the rate of about $200 a month.

He told me that would be satisfactory, then

handed me a blank note form. "Fill this out," he said, "for $1,000, payable in thirty days. When it matures, pay us $200 and make a new note for $800. Do that each month until the debt is wiped out."

I need not point out that it was a profitable transaction for me. The bank charged me .5 per cent a month interest. The first month, therefore, I paid $5, the second month, $4, and so on until the last month when the debt was down to $200. Then I had to pay only $1. Altogether I paid $15 for the accommodation. But the 5 per cent discount that I earned on my merchandise bills amounted to $50. I gained a clear $35 by using bank credit.

To this day I do not know why the bank considered me good for the loan. Mr. Willett did not ask me for a financial statement, nor had I been called on by a Dun or Bradstreet representative. I had been in business less than a year. The only explanation I can give is that I was careful always to keep a balance in bank, no matter how small it might be. I never gave a check that wasn't covered. None of my wholesalers had ever made a draft on me. Perhaps, too, it was in my favor that my store was only a little way up the street and the cashier passed every day on his way to and from the bank. I made my window displays as attractive as possible, and, though I employed a clerk, I always opened up in the morning and locked up at night. Often I went back after dinner to work on my books and straighten stock. Possibly Mr. Willett considered such energy the mark of a rising young business man.

A couple of years after negotiating my first bank loan, Mr. Willett handed me a bit of sound advice that seems worth repeating. I planned to enlarge my store and install a rather expensive set of fixtures. By then I had overcome my inferiority complex, and went confidently to the bank to borrow the sum I needed. As before, Mr. Willett asked what I wanted the money for. When I told him, he remarked that store fixtures were a permanent investment; they did not bring any direct returns. How did I figure I could pay for my projected improvements?

I told him I was doing well and that my store profits would easily take care of the expenditure. He shook his head. "It's highly dangerous," he said, "to count on future profits to pay debts. There may not be any profits!"

I was glad enough later that he did not accommodate me. Newport News depended largely on its shipbuilding industry. There was a slump in shipbuilding and several thousand men were let out of employment. While the slump lasted I did barely enough business to pay expenses. Had I gone into debt for my elaborate fixtures I might have found myself in serious trouble.

When a business man chooses a bank connection it is very important that he choose a bank where the executive head has a practical knowledge of the industry in which the business man happens to be engaged. Every trade has certain peculiarities that a banker must know if he is to serve adequately his customers in that trade. If you are an antique-furniture dealer, for example, it would be unwise for you to choose a bank that serves principally stock raisers or oil-well operators. Or if you are a manufacturer of women's dresses you would not want to patronize a bank that caters mainly to the wholesale grocery trade.

On one occasion I was talking with a prominent building contractor who does business throughout Louisiana and East Texas, when he told me he was about to take his account away from the bank he had done business with for a number of years. It seemed the president of the bank, who had a fair knowledge of the contracting trade, had retired; his successor was a local financier who had made a fortune as a private banker, loaning money on ranch properties.

The contractor had received his money for a

building job a day or two previously and went to the bank to straighten out his obligations. In the course of conversation with the new president the latter made this remark: "Your line of work, Mac, certainly is Greek to me. I don't for the life of me see how you can gamble on these big construction jobs without knowing whether you are going to win or lose."

My contractor friend considered the banker a dangerous man for him to do business with. He did not relish being called a gambler. He is an experienced engineer, graduate of a well known technical school. He does not take a construction job blindly. Yet occasionally some complication occurs that requires immediate cash. The former bank president, being familiar with his operations, would advance the necessary amount without quibbling. But the new president, who thinks the contracting business a gamble, might refuse the accommodation.

Some years ago I had occasion to interview a man in St. Paul, Minnesota, who was in the fur-manufacturing business in a rather large way. He operated in the city a de luxe retail fur store that handled high-priced garments. He also did business with retail merchants in the St. Paul trade territory who bought less expensive goods. While I was in conversation with the fur dealer, he told his secretary it was time to make the bank deposit and not to depend on a street-car, but to take a cab. The fur dealer explained to me that the bank was a good half-mile away, on the opposite side of the city. He said he patronized that particular bank because the loan officer was formerly credit man for a fur concern.

The fur manufacturer had a peculiar credit problem. He began to borrow from the bank in early summer when he started to fabricate garments for his autumn sales. It was necessary to have a good stock on hand by September, when country merchants came to the city to do their buying. But the country merchants required long credit on their purchases; they did not move much of the merchandise until cold weather, and even then put a great many sales on their books. So the manufacturer had to wait for his money. Sometimes a country merchant would settle in January, but often the settlement was not made until February or March.

It was much the same with the fur manufacturer's trade in his fashionable retail store. Persons who purchased garments that cost from $1,000 upward, were apt to be slow pay, as is often the case with the very rich. Having no financial worries of their own, they assume no one else has worries. The manufacturer told me of one charge account against a wealthy family that ran into five figures and had stood on his books two years. He couldn't press for payment for fear of giving offense and losing the family's custom.

Because of slow collections the manufacturer sometimes was not able to clear up the debts he incurred in July until the following April or May. That is why he did business with the bank on the other side of the city, where the loaning officer was an ex-fur man. Knowing the intricacies of the fur business, the loaning officer was not disturbed if now and then the manufacturer needed extra time to meet his obligations.

I chance to know the details of a transaction where a man came to grief from dealings with a banker who did not understand the industry the man was engaged in. It was in Idaho, directly after the 1929 business crash. Idaho's principal industry is sheep raising. Sheepmen winter their flocks in valleys in the southern part of the state and in the spring trail them to the Government-owned pasture land in the northern mountain sections. The industry requires considerable financing, for a sheep owner comes into funds only when he sells his wool and lambs.

During the prosperous years preceding 1929 many Idaho sheepmen made a practice of borrowing from large eastern banks, where they paid a smaller rate of interest than local bankers demanded. When the business slump came on, and prices of wool and lambs sank to low levels, some sheepmen had difficulty in meeting their obligations. One man of my acquaintance could not meet his note at the eastern bank when it fell due. An executive of the bank happened to be in Denver at the time, and the bank wired him to go to Idaho and take the matter in charge.

Doubtless the bank had men on its staff who understood the sheep industry, but the executive who came from Denver was not one of them; he was an industrial expert, but his knowledge of sheep was somewhat less than nothing. Arriving at Pocatello, he called on a local banker for advice. He had in his hand a week-old telegram that read, "Take charge of So-and-So's band of four thousand ewes." The first question the easterner asked was, "What is an ew-ey?"

The Pocatello banker explained that an ewe is a lady sheep, and that the band was out on the range trying to keep alive on sagebrush. It was the dry season, and the owner had no money to buy feed. On sagebrush sheep can keep alive, but that is about all: the wool curls up; it is not good for the coming crop of lambs. When the ewes were finally sold they brought $1 apiece, which was not enough to pay the owner's bank debt. Had he borrowed from a local banker who understood the sheep industry, the banker for his own protection would have had the band properly looked after. Even in that depression year the ewes would have brought several times the amount they actually sold for.

In the small settlement of Buffalo, Kentucky, my friend Mr. E. S. Ferrill is a very successful banker and wholesale merchant. Though Buffalo has fewer than four hundred people, Mr. Ferrill does a merchandise business of $1,500,000 a year, selling to retail storekeepers throughout the western portion of Kentucky. As a banker he is equally successful. Farmers and business men of half a dozen surrounding counties keep their deposits in his bank and come to him for loans.

Mr. Ferrill had no formal bank training. As a youth of twenty he came to the village with capital of $400, earned by farm labor, and bought a small, run-down store that had sales of less than $10 a day. As his business grew he branched out into wholesaling; then, as there was no bank in the village, he began to accept deposits from customers and became a regular banker.

Recently a Louisville newspaper commented editorially on Mr. Ferrill's career and stated, "Mr. Ferrill is successful because he has mastered the problems of his area."

Doubtless that is true, though Mr. Ferrill himself puts it into simpler language. The majority of his banking customers are farmers. He says he has been successful as a farmer banker because he worked on farms as a youth and gained a practical knowledge of the farming industry.

Mr. Ferrill believes it is good business for a banker to promote the prosperity of his customers even at the sacrifice of immediate banking profit. He has certain rules for farmer loans. Though he carries farm tractors in his merchandise stock, he will not loan money to a farmer for the purchase of a tractor if the farmer owns less than one hundred and fifty acres. He counsels such a farmer to continue to use horses. He tells him his farm can not profitably support a tractor.

Mr. Ferrill has another rule to which he strictly adheres. The territory around Buffalo is good grass land, and in early spring farmers come to the bank for loans with which to buy cattle that they turn out to pasture and sell in the fall. There is generally a fair profit to be made if the farmer operates conservatively. Mr. Ferrill's idea of conservatism is that a man with a one-hundred-acre farm should not try to fatten more than twelve head. If a one-hundred-acre farmer plans to buy more than twelve, Mr. Ferrill tells him it is a gamble, and refuses the loan. Because, unless it happens to be an exceptionally favorable season, the farmer will have to buy feed. When he does that he is likely to lose money.

Mr. Ferrill is a constructive banker. Now and then some would-be borrower considers him too conservative, yet farmers who deal with him are more than ordinarily prosperous. There was a far smaller percentage of farm foreclosures during the long depression of the 1930's in his territory than in other parts of the South.

· CHAPTER V ·

How Much Shall I Owe?

EVERY YEAR in the United States thousands of new businesses are started. Some years the number goes as high as one hundred thousand. The majority of men who start new businesses do so on limited capital—store clerks who have saved some money and open stores of their own; inventors who have patented mechanical contrivances and start shops to manufacture them; traveling salesmen who quit traveling to open wholesale businesses and sell to their old customers. And to every person who starts a new business this question arises: Shall I start on a small scale with what capital I have and work up slowly? Or, shall I use my credit and start on a bigger scale?

Suppose we analyze the good and bad features of both procedures. I am, let us say, a clerk in a stationery store and have a couple of thousand dollars, either saved from my wages or left me by a kind relative, with which I plan to go into business. I decide that I will not owe any money. I will pay cash for my goods and sell for cash only. But my $2,000 is scarcely enough to buy a very impressive stock of goods. I could hardly afford to open up on Main Street where my rent would be $200 or $300 a month, to say nothing of the expense of an impressive Neon sign and elaborate show-cases and wall cabinets to match those of my Main Street neighbors. By the time I paid for my sign and fixtures and gave my landlord a month's rent in advance, I wouldn't have any money left to buy my stock.

My only chance would be to rent a small store on a side street where my rent would not be more than $50 a month. I would buy inexpensive fixtures. Probably I would have to get along without a clerk at first. Whatever profits I made I would plow right back into my business. Eventually I might attract a sufficient number of regular customers and increase my stock to the point where I could move up to the high-rent Market Street district. But it would be slow work and not a very exciting life. I couldn't be active in the Chamber of Commerce, and I would never be mentioned in the newspapers as a Leading

Merchant. The main advantage of it would be that I could always feel safe.

Now let us suppose that I didn't want to start in such a humdrum manner. With my knowledge of the stationery business and my acquaintance with salesmen for wholesale firms, I could easily buy a part of my stock on credit. I would buy $5,000 worth of merchandise, of which $2,000 would actually be mine; the other $3,000 I would be in debt for. I would buy my fixtures and my Neon sign on instalments. Thousands of businesses are started that way. If I turned out to be an exceptionally skilful merchandiser I could possibly stand the expense of a Market Street location and in time work off my debts. Yet the chances are I wouldn't be as happy as though I had started in a more modest way. I might go along swimmingly as long as times were good; but then a depression might come along, or there would be a strike in the railroad shops, or a drought in the surrounding country, and my sales would fall off a third or even one-half. My rent and the wages of my clerks would be going on just the same. After paying my running expenses there would be very little left to send to the wholesale firms that I owed. I would write explaining local conditions and wholesalers would probably be lenient with me, but, after all, debts are debts, and some creditors would begin to want more than promises. They would decline to ship me any goods except on a cash-in-advance basis. Occasionally a wholesaler would allow me to settle my account with a ninety-day note. That would relieve me for the time being, though I would have to pay interest on the note, which would increase my expenses just that much more. Eventually things would pick up and I would get on my feet again. But the question is, would I get enough pleasure out of my big Market Street store to pay for the worries I went through?

There is an in-between way of financing a new business, neither so conservative as the first nor so venturesome as the second example I have cited. It is to use your credit, but to a moderate degree. You can find out what a moderate degree is by consulting the man in your town who represents one of the big credit-rating organizations. He will tell you that if you have, say, $10,000, and you are in debt only $3,000, his organization will give you a rating of A-1. With that rating you can place an order for supplies anywhere and suppliers will ship your orders without question.

If, with the same $10,000 capital, you stretch your indebtedness to $5,000, the credit organization won't be quite so flattering. You will get a rating of A-2. Suppliers would still ship your ordinary orders, but if an order happened to be for an extra large amount, the supplier might want to investigate a little before making the shipment.

If you decide to make a still bigger splash on your $10,000 capital and to start in with a $20,000 investment—which means that you would owe $10,000 —then the credit-rating organization won't venture to rate you at all. Opposite your name in the rating book there will be a symbol that indicates, "Your credit is problematical." If you send an order to some supplier, he is likely to write back that he appreciates your business but would like to have cash before making shipment.

You may think it is pretty arbitrary of the credit-rating organization to deny you a rating because your debts amount to as much as your capital. You may reason: "Suppose I do owe $10,000. My assets are that much greater. I've got a $20,000 business instead of a $10,000 one. My original capital is there, no matter what I owe. So why should I be denied a rating?"

The trouble is, all sorts of eventualities have to be taken into account. In the first place, when your debts are as much as your capital, you don't exactly own your business. Your creditors are equal partners with you.

Then there is a still more serious reason for your blank rating. Perhaps you figure that your business is worth $20,000 because it inventoried that much when you started it. But that isn't the case. It may be worth $20,000 to you, but not to any one else. Suppose something happens that makes it necessary to turn it into cash at short notice. How much will it bring?

If it were an old-established business with a good record of earnings, it might bring one hundred cents on the dollar. But we are talking about a new business, not yet well established. Closing out such a business generally brings pretty sad returns.

Suppose it is a retail business. You advertise a closing-out sale and at first you make out pretty well. You get cost out of your goods, or even better. But when the most salable things are exhausted and you come down to broken lots, you make some pretty heavy sacrifices. Yet the expense of your sale keeps right on. And at the very end you have to dispose of the rag, tag, and bobtail to job-lot dealers for anything you can get.

When it is all over and you have paid the expenses of the sale, you are lucky to realize $.50 on the dollar. I have known closing-out sales to net as little as one-third inventory price. So you can figure out why, if you start your business with your debts equaling your capital, the credit-rating organization might give you a blank rating. If you realize $.50 on the dollar, there is just enough to pay your creditors, but nothing for yourself. And if you realize less than $.50 on the dollar, there isn't even enough to pay the creditors.

If the business that you are starting happens to be in the manufacturing line, with the bulk of your investment in special machinery, the close-out can be even worse than in a mercantile business. Among my acquaintances there is a man in New York City who started a small plant to fabricate certain metal specialties. Within a year after he started, he had a long spell of illness and thought he would have to quit. It was fortunate he didn't have to, because for machinery that cost him $6,000, the best offer he could get was $750.

I believe men who are starting in business are apt to place too much emphasis on the amount of capital they have, or haven't. Generally a man goes into business for just one purpose: to provide himself with a permanent job. Thousands of men quit salaried positions every year to strike out for themselves because in the back of their minds is the constant fear that their positions may go out from under them. A man who starts out for himself and makes a go of it, is generally one who faces the fact that it must be a real working job. The capital that he puts into his business is just a tool to work with.

Suppose we consider again the $10,000 capital we have been talking about. It is quite a sizable sum. But it isn't enough to entitle you to be an executive and sit in a private office, though I have known a good many men who thought it did.

It is easy enough to figure that out. Suppose some one leaves you a legacy of $10,000. You know that can't support you. Invested at 5 per cent interest, it would earn $500 a year. You couldn't live very high on that. And there is no reason to suppose your $10,000 will automatically earn more because you invest it in some kind of business.

You might say, even, that when you start your own business, you work to support your capital, instead of your capital working to support you.

I knew a young man who learned the trade of making trunks and for a number of years worked in a big retail trunk and leather goods establishment. He made and repaired trunks in a room at the back of the salesroom. He earned good wages and eventually saved about $1,000, with which he planned to start a factory of his own to make trunks for the city retail trade.

The proprietor of the store offered to give him considerable business. The store had a big sale on one special trunk of simple construction; it sold several hundred of them a year, and the proprietor said he would let Henry make them. The trunk retailed at $4, and a reasonable cost of construction was about $2.75.

Henry started his factory in a loft building not

far from the retail establishment and for two or three months seemed to do all right, turning out these special trunks for his former employer and doing order work and repairs for other dealers in the city. But one day he went to his former employer and said he was losing money on making the $2.75 trunk, he would have to get at least $3.50 for it. His $1,000 capital was all gone and he didn't have any money to buy materials with.

The merchant told him it would be impossible to pay $3.50; the established retail price was $4, and a profit of $.50 wasn't enough to cover the store's overhead and delivery expense. He went over to Henry's factory to see what might be the trouble.

One look showed him where the trouble was. Henry employed two workmen, a journeyman trunk maker, and a boy apprentice. Henry believed his business should support him instead of his supporting his business. He had fixed up a platform with a railing around it at one end of the room where he sat at a desk wearing a white collar and watched his workmen at their tasks. When the merchant said that wasn't the way to make a go of his factory, Henry replied stubbornly, "But I'm a business man now. I'm not supposed to work with my hands."

The last I heard of Henry he had quit the trunk-making industry as a bad job and was learning the plumber's trade.

If you dig into the histories of really big American businesses, you will find that most of them were started by men who went along on what capital they had and didn't use their credit until they knew pretty well where they were going. The founder of Hires Root Beer was a Philadelphia druggist who manufactured his product in the back room of his store. One day on a street-car he met the owner of one of the Philadelphia newspapers who suggested that the sale of the product might be increased by judicious advertising. Mr. Hires answered that he didn't have any spare cash and was opposed to going into debt.

The newspaper owner told him: "If you want to advertise in my paper you needn't pay me until the advertising has brought in enough extra money to pay the bill." When Mr. Hires finally said he was ready to settle, his advertising bill was $700. It was the first debt ever contracted for the beverage that now is vended in every corner of the country, with sales running into the millions.

I think about the best advice on the use of credit was given a young farmer friend of mine in the upper part of New York State. The family place of two hundred acres that George inherited was an apple farm for two or three generations; then, a few winters ago, a long sub-zero spell ruined the trees completely.

George turned to dairying. He already had three or four milch cows, and bought enough more to bring his herd up to ten. He raised his own feed, so the ten cows earned enough, together with the wheat and beans George produced, to meet family expenses in spite of the loss of his orchards. But then the Second World War came along and a new complication set in. Farm help became difficult to get as young men of the neighborhood quit their jobs to go to work in defense industries. The farm had always required the work of two hired men, plus the work of the owner, to keep things going. But the best George could do was to sign up one hired man for a year's contract.

The work of milking ten cows morning and evening, along with carrying out the sanitary regulations that New York State insists on, just about used up all the hired man's time. George, unfortunately, has weak wrists and is no good at milking. He couldn't raise much in the way of cash crops, working by himself. It was nip and tuck to keep the farm out of the red.

George thought of a way out. He reasoned that if ten cows earned a profit, twenty cows would earn twice as much. He would buy ten more cows and go into dairying exclusively. He would build a new stable and equip it with such sanitary arrangements that no state milk inspector could ever find any fault. Then he would install an electric milking machine that would cut down the hired man's milking time by half.

But he didn't have any money. He went to the village bank to see about a loan. The bank president, a successful ex-farmer, considered George's request a few minutes. Then he said, "Yes, I *could* loan you $3,000, and take a mortgage on your farm as security. But I'd kind of hate to do that. A mortgage, you know, has a disagreeable way of sticking around longer than you figure it ought to. Like a distant cousin, you might say, who comes for a week's visit and stays the rest of his life."

"But I'd be able to pay off the mortgage in two or three years," George said. "I figure my twenty cows would earn more than $100 a year apiece. It would be clear profit because I'd raise all my own feed."

"Unless there happened to be a big drought," the banker interrupted. "In that case you'd have to buy feed at a pretty high price. Then your cows wouldn't earn much of anything. There's something else to think about, too. To double the size of your herd, you'd have to go out and buy cows from other dairymen. And dairymen, you know, aren't generally anxious to sell their best producers.

You might pay from $100 to $150 for a cow and she'd turn out to be a liability instead of an asset."

"I guess I'd have to take a chance on that," George told him. "I'm barely keeping my head above water, the way it is now. Last year I actually ran behind."

The banker interrupted again. "Maybe you're forgetting," he said, "the $180 interest you'd have to pay the bank for the money you want to borrow. You'd have to pay that whether you earned it or not. You'd be taking a chance, all right." He twiddled his thumbs a minute or two, then went on: "No, George, I won't slap a mortgage on your farm, but I'll give you some free advice. Get along the best you can for a while. Let the hired man spend his time on the stock while you yourself buckle down and raise what cash crops you are able with your own work. Leave the future to your cows. A cow, you know, is about the most matrimonial creature there is. Let her follow her own inclinations and she'll produce a calf every year, regular as clock work. Keep that up, and it won't be long before you'll have your twenty head without spending a dollar. By then you ought to have enough money saved up to pay part cash for your new stable and fixings. A $1,000 debt won't hurt you. If you need that, there won't be any bother about a mortgage. I'll lend it to you on your personal note."

CHAPTER VI.

The Credit Profession

WHAT QUALIFICATIONS must a man have to be a good credit executive? The most intelligent answer to that question I have ever heard was once given me by the veteran president of a great New York banking institution. The banker is frequently called upon to make speeches before groups of men in different parts of the country who are connected with banking. Almost always at the end of a session, the banker told me, young men come to him to say:

"I've worked for years in such-and-such a bank. There doesn't seem to be any future for me. I'm in a rut. What in the world can I do to get out of it?"

After a five-minute conversation, the banker told me, it is fairly easy to understand why a young man is in a rut. Some young men simply are not smart enough to be pushed ahead toward the job of cashier or loaning officer. But much more frequently it is not lack of brains but lack of courage, that holds men back. They are afraid to take responsibility. Never will such a man make a suggestion for fear he may be held responsible for its success. Responsibility is the one thing he is afraid to face.

A man who passes on credits for a manufacturing or wholesaling corporation has even more need for courage than a banker. His job has more ramifications, more uncertainties. Nearly always when a banker has to make a decision on a loan, he sits face to face with the applicant. He gets his information at first hand. He learns what the applicant intends to do with the money in case the loan is made. If necessary he can go to the applicant's place of business to investigate how the business is conducted.

But the commercial credit executive works mostly at long range. A merchant who orders a bill of goods and expects credit terms of thirty, sixty, or ninety days, may be a thousand miles away. All the credit executive has to go on is a report in the rating book of a credit-rating agency, along with some information gained from other suppliers from whom the merchant has made purchases. The report of the salesman who took the order may also be taken into account. But salesmen are naturally inclined toward optimism. A man who has worked hard to make a sale does not like to take chances that his efforts may be nullified by negative action at the home office.

A good credit executive is born, not made. I could mention the name of a very important New England manufacturing corporation that has had sad experience with credits from the assumption that a man may modify the temperament with which nature has endowed him. The corporation had three credit executives in as many years, all failures. Number one was a gentleman who held the post for many years with reasonable success. But as age crept on, the executive developed a surprising streak of pessimism; to put it plainly, he became so finicky and so insistent on customers living up to rules of his own making that he lost some of the corporation's best accounts.

He was retired on a pension and his assistant promoted to the position. The assistant lasted only a few months. His handicap lay in the fact that his entire experience had been in routine office work. He was lacking in general business knowledge. Like his predecessor he wrote sharp letters to customers.

The corporation directors decided to try out a man of entirely different temperament. There was a star salesman who had a remarkably fine record. He was expansive, friendly, and very popular with customers on the territories he covered. From his long experience on the road, and his intimate contacts with buyers, he had an understanding of customers' problems. The directors believed he would be exactly the man to handle credits.

But immediately the star salesman took his new post he became a changed man. Apparently he conceived the idea that expansiveness and geniality were unsuited to a credit executive. And, like so many other men who try to go against their born tendencies, he overplayed the rôle. One of the things he insisted on was that no customer should be allowed a cash discount if remittance was received later than the ten-day discount period. He took no account of a customer's financial responsibility or former correct paying habits. Rules were rules. He had been in office but a short time when a check came in from one of the corporation's best customers, an old-established firm in Rochester, New York, that had a triple-A rating and a country-wide reputation for fairness. The check was two days late. The firm had taken the cash discount. The recently created credit executive mailed the check back with a reproving letter. The firm, true to its habits of fairness, sent a remittance that covered the invoice without taking the discount, and apologized for its error.

The ex-salesman was not so successful in another incident, when he returned the check of a powerful

Chicago concern whose remittance came a day or so late. Instead of sending a new check the concern took up the matter with the corporation's Chicago office, demanding a reason for such high handed treatment. The Chicago office relayed the details back to New England headquarters. The ex-star salesman was relieved of credit work and sent back on the road.

Any one who tries to change the disposition he was born with is tackling a well nigh impossible job, whether he is in credit work or anything else. Whenever I see some one trying to do it I recall the case that occurred in the city where I used to be in business. A rich corporation lawyer decided to run for mayor. He was a stiff, unbending man, who seldom spoke to any one as he walked along a street and when he did speak it was in the condescending manner of a lord of the manor recognizing one of his peasants.

When he began his campaign for the mayoralty he made a prodigious effort to overcome his natural instincts. He managed a smile and waved his hand to people he met whether he knew them or not. One day in company with two henchmen he made a tour of the retail district, stopping to call on the various merchants. His visit to my store was one of the saddest affairs I have ever witnessed. He clapped me on the back, handed me his campaign card and called me his pal. He clapped each of my clerks on the back, and did the same to three or four customers who happened to be in the store. At the doorway as he went out he turned back, wagged a finger, and shouted, gaily, "Don't forget me election day!" I didn't know whether to resent his familiarities or to feel sorry for him. The labor-union man who opposed him for the mayoralty came out ahead by a four-to-one vote.

Though a man may lack some qualifications for first class credit work, he can at least partially make up by cultivating an amiable character. He can be on friendly terms with his associates. In every organization there are bound to be differences of opinion between the credit department and the sales department. The sales manager and the men under him are naturally desirous of a liberal credit policy that will enable them to do a larger volume of business. The credit manager must be intelligently conservative in order to avoid credit losses.

Some time ago I read in *Printers' Ink* an article by Mr. J. H. Warburton, sales manager for the Marietta Chair Company, who frankly discusses this problem. A salesman frequently writes in, Mr. Warburton states, to mention some concern on his territory that "I could do some business with but I'm afraid any order I took would be turned down by our credit department. The concern seems all right to me. Won't you see if the rules can be loosened up a bit?"

When such a letter comes in, Mr. Warburton shows it to Mr. Helker, the credit manager. They have been close friends during the years they have held their respective positions at the factory. Occasionally the credit manager concedes the point; more often he explains in detail just why he can not approve of putting the concern on the factory's books. "I have enough confidence in my friend's judgment," Mr. Warburton writes, "to accept his decision without question. In all these years we have never had a disagreement. Orders pass through my department to his desk and I never see them again."

In another concern with which I am familiar, the credit manager yielded to the frequent requests of the sales manager, backed by petitions from salesmen, to liberalize credits in a certain territory. The salesmen claimed there were many concerns that, while not precisely the best risks, would be able to pay their bills. The salesmen would almost guarantee there would be no losses.

The credit manager agreed to try the experiment for one year. At the end of that time losses in that territory were above 5 per cent. Previously the losses were less than 1 per cent.

The following may seem a strange statement, but

it is true: A manufacturing or wholesale concern that has some credit losses is in a healthier condition than a concern that has no credit losses.

Quite recently a sixty-year-old manufacturing corporation in the food industry discontinued business. Its sales had gradually gone down until there was no profit. The trouble lay in the fact that the corporation fell into the habit of doing business the easy way. In the beginning it sold to all sorts of outlets, big and little. As time went on it gradually dropped the little fellows and concentrated on large wholesale houses. These houses were so well established and so strong financially that there were practically no credit problems. From credit losses that averaged nearly 1 per cent when a good proportion of customers were little fellows, the yearly losses diminished to practically nothing.

It was a comfortable position, but not safe. Every so often some large wholesaler-customer would go out of business, or, perhaps, discontinue the lines it had formerly bought from the manufacturing corporation. When that occurred it left a hole in the corporation's sales volume that was difficult to plug up. Some little fellows whose credit in the beginning had been perhaps a bit shaky, had become prosperous, but they had tied up with suppliers who had nursed them along through the hard years.

There is a subject dealing with credits that I

know to be quite debatable, but worth discussing. I refer to the practice of some manufacturers and wholesalers whereby their salesmen are permitted to solicit orders from concerns without ascertaining in advance whether any orders they get may, or may not get, will be approved by the home-credit department.

I can not believe this to be a good practice. A business man who has ordered a bill-of-goods will certainly not be pleased if later on he receives a letter from the manufacturer's credit department that runs, "We appreciate the order that you gave our Mr. Jones, but we do not feel that your financial condition at present is strong enough to warrant shipment of the goods on our regular terms of credit. Should you care to pay in advance for the merchandise we shall be glad—"

I contend that a merchant who has had that experience must have a disposition of more than ordinary sweetness not to bear resentment. And should he eventually attain a desirable rating, the chances are he will not give business to the house that once turned him down.

Though it illustrates the reverse side of what we have been discussing, I will risk a personal reminiscence. When I opened my first store it was a rather tiny affair, two show-cases and window-display space, with a millinery shop occupying the balance of the room. I had been open only a few days when a salesman came along, followed by a hotel porter carrying two sample cases. He stopped a few minutes to inspect my window display, then came inside and suggested that he had some items I might profitably use. I selected goods to the amount of something like $200. When he finished writing up the order he remarked genially, "I guess you'd like this stuff as soon as possible. I'll tell the firm to ship at once."

His firm was a Providence manufacturer. I expected a letter asking for references, or perhaps advance payment, but none came. Instead, the merchandise arrived within a week, with terms plainly marked, "5 per cent 10 days, 90 days net."

It is scarcely necessary to say that I was favorably inclined toward the Providence manufacturer and bought its products as long as I was in business. Years later the salesman explained that he had an arrangement with the firm to cover just such cases as mine. Whenever he ran across some beginner merchant whom he believed had a chance of success, he would sell the merchant a bill of goods and personally guarantee payment.

The firm paid him a cash bonus on accounts that he guaranteed. When he told me about it, he said he received his cash bonus on my purchases for a number of years, long after I had attained a reasonably good rating in the credit agencies. So long as the firm didn't say anything about it, he didn't feel it was his duty to bring up the subject.

When a firm is engaged in foreign trade it is particularly necessary for the credit executive to take care that no business man shall be offended by a salesman taking an order that can not be shipped. Foreign business men, particularly those of Latin origin, are generally more sensitive than Americans.

At one time several general merchandise wholesalers in the Southwest endeavored to promote sales in Old Mexico, but none had great success. Not realizing the difference in temperament, the assumption was that a salesman who spoke Spanish would be able to sell merchandise in the same manner as was then customary in the United States. At the time it was difficult to get accurate credit information on Mexican, Spanish, and French merchants established below the Rio Grande. A salesman, for example, might take an order from a merchant in Chihuahua, Coahuila, or Sonora; before the Texas concern ventured to ship the merchandise, a more or less reliable report on the merchant had to be obtained from a rating agency in Mexico City, or from some American person in the town where the merchant did business. It was slow work to get the information; by the time the information was at hand, very often the merchant sensed the reason for the delay, considered it a reflection on his honor, and indignantly canceled the order. To use a familiar term, the southwestern wholesalers did not get to first base in Mexico.

All but one. It happened I had a close friend connected with a Texas wholesale concern. He was a young lawyer, who had done some legal work for the concern; that led to full time employment; eventually he became a sort of general factotum—legal adviser, director of sales, and supervisor of credits. The concern's sales were around $3,000,000 annually. My friend believed he saw a chance for expansion below the Rio Grande. He conceived a new form of approach. As a youth he had associated with cultured Spanish and French families in San Antonio; he spoke those languages perfectly and was well versed in Latin social usages.

One week each month he quit his duties at the wholesale house and went on a tour of the northern Mexican states. Arriving at a town, he learned the names and locations of leading merchants, then went to the bank and made discreet inquiries as to various merchants' financial standings. Finally deciding which merchant was the most favorable prospect, he made a personal call, dressed in his most formal attire. His approach went something like this:

"Señor, I am, as you may surmise, an *Americano*. I am in the wholesale business. Yet I have not come to sell. Merely, I visit. But with your permission I would like to mention some lines of our merchandise that you might handle with profit. In a few days one of our salesmen may have the pleasure of calling on you. Should you be pleased to give him an order, I can assure you that the goods will be shipped the very day that the order is received."

Almost invariably the interview resulted in a friendly attitude on the part of the merchant. The *Americano's* manner was similar to that of the representatives of European houses from which the merchant was in the habit of buying. He knew, too, that American merchandise was in many respects more desirable than European. Most of all, the promise that the goods would be shipped without irritating delay while his reliability was being investigated, was gratifying to his *amour propre.*

When the wholesaler's salesman arrived there was little trouble in doing business. In the course of two or three years the Texas wholesale house was annually shipping more than $1,000,000 worth of merchandise to customers south of the Rio Grande.

One problem that a credit executive frequently faces is that of the old customer who has a long record of prompt payments, but who unaccountably becomes slow. Instead of discounting his bills, the customer takes the full time allowed. Even then, perhaps, he does not settle in full, but lets a balance string along, sending a small remittance now and then with vague promises to do better in future. The credit executive hesitates to take drastic action on account of former pleasant relations. The customer may be hard pressed from unusual conditions—crop failures, a strike in the principal industrial plant, or illness in his family that entails large hospital and surgeon's bills.

The credit executive for a Pennsylvania manufacturing concern tells me of a case in his own experience. The lame-duck customer was a medium-sized jobber of electrical goods in Ohio. So far as the credit man could learn, there had been no drought, strike, or illness to cause financial trouble. The credit executive has a procedure that he learned in his youth when he operated a harvesting machine on his father's Minnesota farm. "Four or five small parts," he says, "can cause trouble in a harvesting machine. If you investigate those parts and none of them are out of order, then it's time to send to town for an expert mechanic."

In the case of the Ohio jobber the credit man assumed the rôle of expert and made a trip to the jobber's town. He found it was a weakness for quantity buying that had got the man in trouble. The jobber could not resist the lure of an extra discount. If the price of an appliance was $2.00 each in lots of one hundred and a manufacturer's salesman offered it at $1.90 on a purchase of one thousand, the jobber ordered one thousand. The result was an accumulation of merchandise far beyond what his business warranted. Much of it was out of date. He had got so far behind in payments to suppliers that several were threatening to sue.

The credit man pointed out the error of his ways: "You buy one thousand items so as to gain a 2 per cent discount. Your saving is $20.00. But if you have half the stuff left on your hands, the saving isn't a drop in the bucket compared with your loss."

The only way for the jobber to avoid bankruptcy, the credit man said, was to turn his obsolete stock into cash, even though it brought only ten cents on the dollar, then settle with his most insistent creditors. If the jobber would do that, and promise to curb his passion for quantity buying, the credit man's firm would accept the jobber's notes for his debt, payable in nine, twelve, and fifteen months. Meanwhile, the firm would fill any orders the jobber sent in, on regular terms. The firm was the jobber's largest creditor.

The jobber paid out and eventually got on a discounting basis. The credit executive did a constructive piece of work. He not only got the money that was owing his firm, but kept a customer in business.

At this point I can imagine hearing some credit man's protest: "Oh, yes, that's all very fine, but what has it to do with me? You are talking about big shots—men who are so important they can do as they please. But I'm not a big-shot credit man. I'm just a salaried employee. I wouldn't have authority to go into Old Mexico and extend credit to foreigners on my own judgment, and I couldn't accept a lame-duck merchant's notes in lieu of cash. If I did, and things turned out wrong, I'd probably be out of a job."

My answer to the protest is this: Isn't it, perhaps, your own fault if you lack authority? Neither of the two men I have quoted was important when he started. Each gained importance as he went along. He used the judgment he was endowed with to the best of his ability and had the courage to back his judgment. If he made a mistake he didn't try to shift the blame. He was far more anxious to pass an order than to turn one down. Neither man regarded his work as just a job. It was an important part of the machinery of business.

· CHAPTER VII ·

Selling versus Financing

IF YOU were credit executive for a wholesale or manufacturing concern, and two men, each preparing to start a merchandising business, were to come in and ask for a line of credit—one whose experience had been mainly with selling, and the other with a sound financial background—which would you be most inclined to put on your concern's books?

Perhaps you would favor the salesman, figuring that the retail business is a selling game and that if selling is brisk enough, the financing will pretty well take care of itself. But you might easily be mistaken. If you study the histories of successful businesses you will find the majority were successful from the start because the men who founded them were skilful financiers rather than outstanding salesmen.

The ideal arrangement, of course, is a partnership in which one partner is a super salesman and the other a first-class financial man. There is an old saying current among retailers, "What every store needs is a glad-hander up at the front door and a tightwad back in the office." But few businesses are started with sufficient capital to warrant the expense of two owners' salaries. Often, at the beginning, a business is barely able to support a single owner, particularly if he happens to be a married man with a family on his hands.

It is seldom that a man possesses great sales sense and great financial sense. When he does, he generally goes a long way. Particularly if his financial sense dominates his sales sense. Mr. J. C. Penney, founder of the Penney chain of retail stores, is a rather good example. Some years ago, when Mr. Penney was still active head of his chain, I spent an afternoon with him at his New York headquarters. He impressed me as a conservative man, as far as possible from the "high pressure" salesman type. His father was an Episcopal clergyman. Mr. Penney began his merchandising career in 1902 at Kemmerer, Wyoming, a village of less than two thousand population, with so little money and so meager a stock of merchandise that he could not afford a clerk. His wife helped out part of each day in the store, bringing their baby with her, where it slept in a basket under the counter. That was the origin of the present Penney chain with nearly two thousand branches and annual sales of $250,000,000.

A few months after my New York interview, on a cross-country trip, I chanced to spend a night in Kemmerer, and an old settler spoke to me about the town's best-known alumnus. "No one ever thought he was anything wonderful," the old settler said. "He had a book that he was always figuring in when he wasn't waiting on customers. Two or three other storekeepers around here were a lot livelier salesmen than Penney. He never tried to sell you anything that you didn't want!"

It may be well to analyze the meaning of the word "financial" as applied to merchandising. Many people have an idea that the financial man of a commercial house is one whose entire duties consist of counting up the cash at night, carrying it to the bank next morning, arranging with the banker if possible for loans, and writing checks for payment of bills. A financial man often does those things, of course; but if he is a first rate financial man they are merely small chores subordinate to his main function which is: *to have money in bank to meet bills when they fall due.*

In a southern city there is a very successful clothing firm consisting of two young men who are exceptionally well mated; one was formerly star salesman in a retail clothing store, the other office manager for a wholesale drug house. They started at a most unfortunate time, directly after the 1929 business slump. Their capital of some $7,000 was in a local bank. They had rented a store-room, installed fixtures and placed orders for merchandise with eastern manufacturers, when the bank closed its doors.

In this crisis the financial partner went to another bank where he had done business for the wholesale drug house and described the predicament they were in to the bank president. He had nothing to offer aside from his record in handling efficiently the drug firm's finances. But the bank president agreed to make a loan sufficient to carry the partners along until the affairs of the closed bank were settled. It was a year before that took place, when they received about $.75 on the dollar for their $7,000. The financial partner steered their craft through the following difficult years. Now they have a first-class rating and are the city's leading firm in their line. Recently I asked the financial man how it was that he could step out of the wholesale drug business into a retail clothing store and handle things so well.

"Probably I did better because I didn't know anything about the clothing line," he answered. "My partner took care of the selling and left everything else to me. I concentrated on just one thing, which was, to have money in the bank to pay bills with. Any firm which can do that succeeds.

"I'll try to describe what I did to earn my way. In the first place, I relieved my partner of detail worries so he could put all his energies into selling. He was a remarkably good salesman, and we employed two or three clerks who also knew their business. All the time I had in mind the fact that if we were to have a good credit rating we must be prepared to pay our bills promptly, so I figured out in advance how much we could afford to spend, and still have money on hand at the crucial time. I estimated how much business we were likely to do in a certain season, and told my partner how much merchandise we could safely buy. I decided how much we could afford to spend on advertising, on window decoration, and on improvements; and I held the expenditures strictly down to my estimates. Had I been mixed up in the selling end it is probable I would not have been so uncompromising, because there is always the temptation to plunge when things you are interested in are going splendidly. Very likely we lost a sale now and then by holding our stock down to what I considered a safe inventory; but it was much better to lose a sale occasionally than to fall down at paying time."

In another chapter I state that the United States has a larger percentage of peace-time failures than other countries and give as a reason the greater spirit of optimism that prevails in our country. I might have mentioned a further reason, namely, that with us the tendency has been to develop the strictly selling end of business faster than the financial end. Particularly in retail trade, more men go into business for themselves who have a talent for selling than those who have a talent for financing.

It is not difficult to find the reason. Two boys, let us say, are graduated from high school and both get jobs in the same establishment on Main Street. One of them is handy with figures and is put back in the office to do the simpler jobs of bookkeeping. The other, who mixes easily with people, is put behind the counter to assist in selling. Almost invariably it is the latter who first has a chance to get into business for himself. He becomes acquainted with the spenders of the community and works up a personal following. He enjoys selling. Eventually he thinks he should capitalize his sales ability and have a store of his own. He may not have any money, but he can usually find some one in town to back him; or, as often happens, some wholesale concern that is not getting a satisfactory business in the community starts him up in order to have an outlet for its merchandise.

Sometimes such arrangements turn out profitably, but often they do not. Mere selling ability is a slim foundation on which to build a permanent enterprise. A born salesman is generally impatient of details; office work is a burden. The expansive optimism that made him a good salesman inclines him to be visionary. He is likely to invest too heavily in merchandise, with the result that he becomes burdened with an accumulation of dead stock.

I recall an almost perfect example of what may happen to a man who is a born salesman but lacks other qualifications. It was when I first went into business, and a young man came to our Virginia town to open a book and stationery store. He was from a large near-by city where he had been head salesman in a prominent book and stationery establishment. He was an extaordinarily sociable person; hardly had he been in town a month before he was on friendly terms with all the local business men. His ambition, as he told every one, was to wake up the old town and show what a real book and stationery store was like.

One of his first moves was quite dramatic. He bought five hundred copies of *The Prisoner of Zenda,* a book that had been a best seller several years previously, and that he secured at a sacrifice price. Originally, I believe, it was a $1.50 book. He took a full page in the Sunday morning newspaper to announce to the public that in conformity with his settled policy of giving the Best for the Least, he would offer these books at the sensational price of $.50 per copy. The advertisement closed with the warning, "Only One Book To Each Customer. Come Early and Avoid the Rush!"

Afterward he told me in confidence that his sale had not been a success. He opened his store an hour ahead of time on Monday morning to serve early buyers, but none came. It was, in fact, nearly noon when the first interested person appeared. A lady stopped to inspect the huge display of *The Prisoner of Zenda* in his show window, then entered the store and asked to see a copy. "I don't want to buy it," she said, "because I already have one. I just wanted to see if these $.50 books are as good as mine." In something less than a year the young bookseller's store was closed, and a sheriff's notice pasted on the front door.

I know how difficult it is for a man who is a born salesman to bury his nose in a set of books. He likes to be up at the front of his store, or even out on the sidewalk, to make himself agreeable with possible buyers. It seems a waste of time to be back in the office fussing with figures. But a retailer should keep an adequate set of books; a retail business is a very complicated affair. The stock is shifting day by day. If a man doesn't keep an exact record of what he buys, which lines of merchandise are selling, and which are sticking to the shelves, he is likely to find his affairs in a rather hopeless state.

As I say, such work is terribly difficult for a man who is by nature a salesman. But it can be managed if he is sufficiently determined. There is the case of my old friend, Mr. George M. Davis, who worked up a business of $250,000 a year in his general store at Rock Glen, a cross-roads settlement in western New York state. Mr. Davis began his career as clerk in another country store and managed to save $1,100, when he decided to go into business for himself. He scarcely knew the difference between a day book and a ledger; in fact he had a decided distaste for figures; but some one told him he should learn to keep a set of books before attempting to operate a store, so he spent a part of his money on a course at a Rochester business college.

The last time I saw Mr. Davis he told me it was the most profitable investment he ever made. Though he had then been in business fifty years, and enjoyed selling as much as ever, he found time between customers to put in a couple of hours each day on his books. He said the work was nothing compared with the satisfaction of knowing exactly how his business stood. In his $40,000 stock there was practically no shop-worn or out-of-date merchandise. He kept substantial balances in three banks in near-by towns and paid for every shipment of merchandise within three days after the arrival of the goods. His rating in the Dun and Bradstreet book was something to be envied.

I have known more than one case where a merchant did exceptionally well in the beginning, but after a few years became less prosperous and sometimes failed completely. The merchant did not grow with his business. It was often the result of too great salesmindedness.

One example comes to my mind that will explain my meaning. A young man of my acquaintance opened a haberdashery store in the good-sized Pennsylvania town where he was born and where he had a wide acquaintance. The first year his sales amounted to more than $25,000, which yielded a good profit because his expenses were down to a minimum. His only employee was a porter who did the cleaning up and ran errands; the young merchant did all the selling. In his newspaper advertisements he always had a picture of himself in the upper left-hand corner of the space with a printed line underneath stating that he welcomed his friends at his store and that his motto was Personal Service.

The trouble with his methods lay in the fact that

he tried to give his friends too much personal service. As his business grew he enlarged his store and employed two or three clerks at liberal salaries. But he never gave his clerks a chance. Whenever customers came in the store the merchant dashed forward to wait on them personally. If a clerk did manage to get hold of a customer, the merchant would often step up and take over the transaction. This was so discouraging to the clerks that they got into the habit of standing about idly or busying themselves in straightening out the goods left on the counters by their employer in his active salesmanship. It was an extravagant state of affairs because he was paying good salaries for work that any errand boy could have done just as well.

When the receiver in bankruptcy took hold of the business he found the back office in a badly disordered state, for the merchant had never been able to take time from his personal service to give his office work attention. There was not even a complete record of all the debts except in the form of invoices hung about on hooks. I happened to know the receiver and remember a remark he made: "This fellow might have got on all right except he was so heated up over being a salesman that he forgot he was a merchant!"

When a man starts a merchandising business and wishes to buy goods on credit, it goes without saying that the manufacturer or wholesaler to whom he applies makes an adequate investigation to learn if he is a desirable customer. The new merchant should do the same thing. Before tying up with any manufacturer or wholesaler, he should make some investigations with this question in mind: "Are the majority of retailers, who are about in my same position, and who do business with this manufacturer or wholesaler, doing well?"

Several years ago a young man opened a retail specialty business in a New England manufacturing town. He had for a number of years been employed as salesman in an old established retail house in Boston, and when he got ready to go into business he naturally thought of buying his merchandise from one of the wholesale concerns that did business with his employers. The wholesale concern was located in New York and the young man went there to make his buying arrangements.

The executives of the concern were exceptionally cordial. His record with the Boston retail house was known to them, and when it came to discussing credit they surprised him by their liberal attitude. The arrangement they proposed was this: The young merchant should buy his opening bill from them, selecting all the merchandise he thought he might need. If he felt he should have any lines they did not carry they would buy such goods for him and charge on their account. In return he was to pay them what money he had, and the balance would be billed on open account with the understanding that he would remit from time to time such amounts as he was able.

The young merchant accepted the proposal, feeling elated over a situation that gave him the backing of an old-established house along with practically unlimited credit. And from almost every angle it was a good arrangement for him. He was spared the necessity for establishing credit with a number of houses, and his financial worries were lessened, because he had only to send in what money he was able from time to time to make everything satisfactory. It was understood, of course, that this easy arrangement was not to be a permanent thing, but to hold good only until he should get on his feet and be able to pay on regular terms.

The wholesale house entered into this arrangement in good faith, as did also the merchant. But there was one flaw that appeared as time went on. The merchant did not get along so well as he expected.

The reason he did not make better progress was because the merchandise he handled was too high-priced for his community. The wholesale concern catered almost exclusively to large-city trade; what went well with prominent retailers in Boston, New

York, and Philadelphia, did not find ready sale in the New England manufacturing town where the young merchant established his business.

And so the merchant found himself in an embarrassing situation. He was not in position to go out and make other buying connections because he was owing so much to the New York wholesale concern; and in order to keep his credit good with them he had to keep on using their goods. It was nearly five years before the merchant got to the point where he was able to shake himself free from his hampering connection and buy in the open market the goods suitable for his trade. And all his troubles arose from the fact that he had not looked around to see whether his wholesale house was making money for other retailers who were located in towns similar to the one where he chose to go into business.

I have pointed out that many small merchants fail through lack of system. Manifestly, it is impossible for a small merchant to bring the same system to bear in the running of his affairs as is used by the large corporation, yet there are certain fundamental rules that, if observed, will simplify matters a great deal. One most important practice is to save time from details so as to have time for larger matters.

I have a friend who started in the diamond business a few years ago. He had been traveling salesman for a large diamond importing house in New York, and when the house went out of business he decided to go into business for himself, counting on his acquaintance with retail jewelers throughout the country to furnish his market. He had limited capital, but was able to get credit from several large diamond importers. Starting this way, he could not afford to employ high-priced help; he was his own buyer, his own office manager, and his own financier. When he went out on the road to call on customers, the only persons in his office were a couple of young women and an office boy.

Diamonds are a decided luxury line, and on account of slow turnover are generally sold on long credit terms. When my friend bought a bill from an importing house he gave a series of notes, one falling due each month. He was obliged to do business with several importing houses in order to secure the sizes and qualities of diamonds he needed for his own trade. Often three or four notes would fall due the same month. He arranged to have them fall due at different dates, his idea being that in stringing out the payments he would be in better position to take care of the obligations.

That broke in on his time considerably and interfered with his selling trips, because he had to be in his office whenever a matured note was presented, or to go to his bank to take care of it there. One day he called at his bank on such a mission and the vice-president asked him why he didn't have all his notes fall due on one certain day of the month. That would, the vice-president said, save a lot of time and trouble.

The diamond dealer replied that nothing would suit him better, but unfortunately he was no millionaire and he had to string out his payments because his jeweler-customers often paid their bills a little at a time, and if he had to meet all his notes at once he might be caught short.

"Yes, I know a lot of business men figure that way," the banker countered. "But isn't the thing just as broad as it is long? If you save up the money that comes in during a given month you will have just as much to pay with; and certainly your bills aren't any smaller because you string out the payments."

The diamond dealer realized the truth of the banker's logic. But on account of his limited capital he had occasionally to ask a creditor to renew a note for a short time, or to pay a part and let the balance stand. It was always embarrassing to make these requests; he had the feeling that it was easier to make them singly than to bunch them all together at one time. The banker went on:

"If you've got a number of disagreeable little jobs to do," he said, "it's easier to face them all at once than to face them separately. You get them off your mind and then you are free to give your whole attention to other things."

My friend the diamond dealer told me the result of the interview. "I took the banker's advice and arranged that all my obligations should fall due the fifteenth of each month. I gave over that day to financing; every other day I had my whole time for other things. I didn't have to jump back to New York every few days when I was out on a selling trip, as I was obliged to do previously. And after I became used to it I found it was no more worrisome to face half a dozen obligations at one time than to face them in driblets. For several years now I have been preaching this to my own customers, and in every case those who have adopted it have thanked me for the suggestion."

· CHAPTER VIII ·

Dun and Bradstreet, Inc.

WHEN OUR original thirteen Colonies became a country, and the country pushed its western boundary across the Allegheny Mountains, to the Mississippi River, and even beyond, there was created a difficult business problem. In 1803, when President Jefferson negotiated the Louisiana Purchase, the only cities of considerable size were still on the Atlantic seaboard, Boston, New York, Philadelphia, Baltimore. Traders who had gone out into the new West looked to wholesale houses in those cities for their supplies. The traders expected credit accommodation. The problem for the wholesaler was, to know which trader was responsible for his debts and which was not responsible.

The old procedure whereby a country merchant presented a letter of recommendation from the pastor of his village church, or from two or three friends, was a slim foundation on which to trust the distant trader with merchandise to the amount of several hundred, or even several thousand, dollars. The pastor might know the trader to be a law-abiding citizen and a good church member, but the pastor could hardly be expected to evaluate expertly the trader's business ability. And the friends who gave the trader his laudatory letters might have done so merely to do him a good turn. The safe granting of credit was a difficult problem even when a storekeeper was only a hundred miles or so distant; it became tremendously more difficult when the storekeeper was in Ohio, Indiana, or western Kentucky.

The first serious attempt to bring efficiency into the gathering of credit information seems to have been made by Baring Brothers, the great London banking house. Beside their European interests, Baring Brothers had large interests in America. They acted as agents for the United States Government and served as brokers for the sale of Federal, State, and municipal bonds in Britain and on the Continent. They extended credit to business enterprises in American cities. In 1828 the firm engaged a Boston business man, Thomas W. Ward, as its special agent in the United States. Mr. Ward traveled extensively, covering practically the entire country as it then existed. He selected correspondents for Baring Brothers, granted credits to American business houses, collected debts and reported upon general business conditions. During his first three years of activity he is said to have granted commercial credits amounting to $50,000,000. That he was a man of remarkable business judgment is shown by the fact that of seven firms of British merchant-bankers doing business in the United States, Baring Brothers and Company was the only one that emerged from the 1837 panic and ensuing business depression with unimpaired prestige, power, and credit.*

Before Mr. Ward's appointment by Baring Brothers, an occasional wholesale firm in New York or some other wholesale center would send a partner or a trusted employee on a trip to collect accounts and to report on the financial standing of customers and prospective customers. In the year 1827 a New York business man, Sheldon P. Church, began independently to investigate credit standings and to render reports to several large wholesale dry-goods merchants in New York. Some years later, the mer-

* From Roy A. Foulke's *Sinews of American Commerce* (Dun and Bradstreet, Inc., 1941). Other pieces of information in this chapter are also from Mr. Foulke's book.

chants he had been representing formed "The Merchants' Vigilance Association," and appointed Mr. Church as their representative, the expenses of his services being pro-rated among the members. He traveled up and down the coast, ventured into the West to investigate traders in the growing cities of Cincinnati, Louisville, and St. Louis; thence down the Mississippi to New Orleans and other southern communities. Cincinnati was by far the most important city west of the Alleghenies, "Queen of the West," with a population of more than forty thousand. St. Louis was a "roaring hive of frontier industry," whose population had trebled in ten years, and boasted 16,469 souls in 1840.

Mr. Church did not mince words in his credit reports. One, written of a trader in Richmond, Virginia:

> Mr. B——— has been many years in trade here under different phases, is worth nothing, never made anything, and never will; he is impulsive, restless, uneasy, of no judgment or forecast. . . .

Another report from Columbus, Mississippi, in which he quotes opinions of two local business men and a lawyer:

> T——— has lately opened a fresh stock of goods here. The first intimation was that "the New Yorkers have set up a man here, and I would not give ten cents on the dollar for his debts." Another authority: "How

did your neighbor manage to get a stock of goods?" "By the art of hocus-pocus, I reckon." Another: "Were you in business would you sell to Mr. T——— $500 on credit?" Answer: "I wouldn't sell him anything. I wish I could get pay for what he owes me."

Mr. Church then sets down his own views:

Mr. T——— was formerly in a small business here and failed; he was a dissipated loafer for the next few years; for the last year or two has had a little shop here of meal, onions, and bolognas and has kept sober, but has acquired no standing here. I am told his veracity is questionable. If such men are safe, who can be called doubtful? I go for the "right of search," suspecting all strange craft.

Yet though this early credit reporter could be caustic, he could be mellow when he believed conditions warranted mellowness:

Nashville, Tennessee: Mr. S——— has been a long time in the auction and commission business—is an industrious, honest man and has made money. He is regarded safe for all his engagements.

Macon, Georgia: B——— and M——— are going on in their steady, straight, prudent course and are making money; are well off and safe.

Successful though he was as a reporter on credits, one can not help the thought that Sheldon P. Church might have been still more successful had he set his hand to work of a purely literary character. It is a masterly picture, that of the bad Mr. T——— of Columbus, Mississippi, "formerly a dissipated loafer who for the last year or so has had a little shop of meal, onions, and bolognas and has kept sober but has acquired no standing"; and the other picture of the good Messrs. B——— and M——— of Macon, Georgia, "going on in their steady, straight, prudent course and making money." These character descriptions would scarcely be out of place in the works of Mr. Church's great contemporaries, Edgar Allan Poe, Charles Dickens, or Gustave Flaubert, creator of Madame Bovary.

The origin of the world's greatest credit agency, Dun and Bradstreet, Incorporated, stemmed directly from the disastrous panic of 1837. Arthur Tappan and Company of New York had one of the largest wholesale and retail silk and cotton goods businesses in the country. For a number of years this firm sold exclusively for cash; but in line with the optimistic tendencies of the boom times preceding 1837, the firm gradually began to sell on credit, until eventually the greater portion of the sales was put on the books. The firm went down in the business débâcle of 1837 with liabilities of $1,000,000, a staggering sum for those days. The firm was reorganized and creditors accepted notes falling due in six, twelve, and eighteen months, that were met when due.

As result of Arthur Tappan and Company's financial embarrassment and subsequent reorganization, a brother, Lewis Tappan, left the firm and proceeded to set up a credit reporting enterprise that he called The Mercantile Agency. The Tappan brothers already had something of a reputation as credit experts. When the Irish lad, A. T. Stewart, who came to America and set himself up in the dry-goods business, was thought by some business men to be overtrading, he called upon Lewis Tappan "as a fit and proper person, both from integrity and business shrewdness, to look into his accounts and make an impartial report of his pecuniary condition, so as to set all doubts at rest."

Apparently Lewis Tappan found the enterprise basically sound because A. T. Stewart became rich enough to be owner of a white marble mansion at Fifth Avenue and Thirty-fourth Street, "the most splendid residence in the city"; and during the Civil War was able to build his merchandising palace at Broadway and Tenth street, that is still one of New York's show places. In 1892 the building and business were acquired by John Wanamaker, as an extension of his Philadelphia department store. A tablet on the Broadway front bears the inscription, "John Wanamaker, Formerly A. T. Stewart."

Lewis Tappan's Mercantile Agency was planned on much broader lines than anything previously attempted. The activities of Sheldon P. Church, for example, were confined to serving a limited number of wholesale merchants, for whom Mr. Church was the sole traveler and credit investigator. His was a one-man enterprise. Lewis Tappan, on the contrary, visioned a country-wide organization that would collect and analyze credit information on traders of every description and sell the results to all wholesale merchants and manufacturers who extended credit to customers. Lewis Tappan, it might be said, was first to apply the principles of mass production to credit reporting. A wholesaler or manufacturer who subscribed to the Tappan service could secure credit data on customers at much less cost than by sending out personal representatives as had formerly been customary.

In August, 1841, Lewis Tappan began active operations. He had already accumulated a valuable amount of information in the New York area; his next step was to send a circular to individuals in towns and cities throughout the country, inviting them to become his correspondents. In many cases the man he selected was a young lawyer. Over the years the Commercial Agency and its successors had as correspondents numbers of men who in after life became celebrated. Abraham Lincoln was correspondent in Springfield, Illinois; Ulysses S. Grant in Galena at the time he worked in his father's retail hardware and leather store, prior to the outbreak of the Civil War; William B. McKinley, while practising law at Canton, Ohio; and General Lew Wallace, distinguished Civil War officer and author of the enormously popular book *Ben Hur*, at Crawfordsville, Indiana. In Vermont, John Calvin Coolidge was a correspondent for more than fifty years, resigning on the day that his son was inaugurated President of the United States.

Through local correspondents it was possible for the Mercantile Agency to secure intimate, unbiased reports on traders that would enable New York wholesalers to decide what amount of credit, if any, could safely be granted—a much more efficient system, it must be admitted, than that of the old days when a country merchant asked for credit on the strength of a letter of recommendation from the merchant's pastor, or some personal friend.

The system was also more efficient than that of Sheldon P. Church, in his travels from place to place. A trader might be financially sound at the time of Mr. Church's interview, but through some mishap be a very doubtful credit risk three months later. Lewis Tappan's agency, on the contrary, was in position through resident correspondents to furnish subscribers up-to-date information of any changes that might occur.

In 1851, completing its first decade of existence,

the Mercantile Agency employed thirty persons at its New York headquarters and maintained branch offices in Boston, Philadelphia, Baltimore, Cincinnati, and Saint Louis. Credit reports were all copied in longhand, in the beautiful Spencerian style that in those days was so highly cherished. The typewriter was a gadget still more than twenty years in the future.

In 1859 young Robert Graham Dun, thirty-two years of age, son and grandson of Scottish-born clergymen, became sole owner of the Mercantile Agency, after being a partner for some years. He changed the name of the enterprise to R. G. Dun and Company, a name that continued until 1933—more than seventy years.

Meanwhile the Mercantile Agency had acquired a competitor. In 1850, Cincinnati was the undisputed business metropolis west of the Alleghenies. Even back in the eighteen-thirties its reputation as a city of unlimited opportunities had traveled across the Atlantic Ocean. Mrs. Frances Trollope, widely known English author and mother of the still more widely known author Anthony Trollope, came to Cincinnati to make her millions in trade. Blandly confident that Americans were wistfully eager to buy goods made in the "Mother Country," Mrs. Trollope erected a building that was to be a depot for English merchandise, consigned by English manufacturers. But apparently middle-west Americans were not overly eager for English goods, nor were English manufacturers eager to risk their goods so far from home on uncertain terms of sale. The authoress' plan fell flat. She retrieved a good part of her losses, however, by publishing a book of severely caustic criticism, *Domestic Manners of the Americans.*

Yet Cincinnati was the springboard from which one local merchant sprang into country-wide prominence. John M. Bradstreet operated a small dry-goods store for nearly twenty years, during which time he made a study of commercial credit problems. Eventually he relinquished his retail business and began the practice of law. One piece of business that came his way was the settling of the affairs of a large insolvent estate. In the course of this work he gained a mass of information concerning the moral and financial responsibilities of business men in the mid-west area; and this, together with the credit data collected during his dry-goods-store years enabled him, in 1849, to set up a credit reporting bureau similar to the one started by Lewis Tappan in New York eight years earlier. By 1855, Mr. Bradstreet's operations were sufficiently successful to warrant the opening of a New York office under the name of Bradstreet's Improved Commercial Agency. From then until 1933, when R. G. Dun and Company acquired the business of the Bradstreet Company, the two firms were active competitors, often opening offices in the same cities, employing credit reporters who called on the same business firms and printing reference books that contained corresponding information. Both companies had gradually come to depend less on local correspondents and to employ an increasing number of full-time traveling reporters. The correspondent served a basic function; but his best service became an auxiliary to the organized efforts of these full-time, trained men, skilled interpreters of credit information.

For a long time mercantile agencies in the eyes of the courts remained in a probationary stage. The courts hesitated to accept this innovation in business activity before the agencies had demonstrated their economic usefulness. Many merchants regarded it as an unjustifiable intrusion on their private affairs that a commercial agency should issue opinions on their financial responsibility and make these opinions known to subscribers. Suits for libel were not infrequent.

In one such case John B. and Horace Beardsley of Norwalk, Ohio, were the complainants. The suit was tried in 1851, in the United States District Court in New York City. In one of the final hearings Charles O'Conor, a prominent lawyer who was later active in the exposure of the notorious "Tweed Ring," made a remarkably lucid explanation of the need of credit reporting in behalf of his client, the Mercantile Agency:

What is the operation of these agencies? The country dealer who comes to any of the cities needs some evidence that he is worthy of trust and confidence. The ancient practice was for the country dealer to bring with him a certificate of his minister of the Gospel, or a letter from some country lawyer, or, perhaps, from some fellow merchant; and then he would spend a week, perhaps, in New York, trying to satisfy the persons with whom he dealt that he was worthy of credit—in establishing for himself, as well as he could, a good character. What has been the result of establishing these agencies? Why, a merchant from this little town of Norwalk, Ohio, walks into the store of the wholesale merchant in New York, or Boston, or Philadelphia, and says: "I should like to purchase from you such and such goods." The city merchant replies: "Well, Sir, look at our goods and whatever you desire to purchase shall be laid aside for you." After spending perhaps half an hour in making his examination and selection of goods, he goes back to the desk of the counting room to talk about terms of payment and credit, etc. He asks, "How long a credit do you allow?" The answer is, "Well, we give four or six months." "Do you require an endorser?" "No, Sir." This answer if the country merchant knew nothing about what is going on in the business world might very much surprise him for perhaps he never was in the store before, and so far as he can tell, he is wholly unknown there. He gets his goods and goes home. He is independent of lawyer and minister and everybody else, so far as this world's mere temporal interests are concerned. Upon the strength of his good character, if he has one, he gets credit. A person of doubtful reputation gets a different answer.

This whole thing is done with a promptitude which is amazing and to all honest people in the country very delightful. They find that indeed that "a good name is better than precious ointment," and "rather to be chosen than great riches"; that it accompanies them everywhere. And all this is through the action of these mercantile agencies. While the country merchant is looking at the goods, the mercantile agency reports that he is a man perfectly worthy of confidence, and upon the strength of this report the New York merchant is willing to trust him; and he does so with a pleasantly confiding manner, which is as gratifying to the pride of the country dealer as it is conformable to propriety.

In the early days credit reporters often had difficulty in persuading business men to give financial statements. Many men angrily refused. There was something of the same attitude that bank examiners encountered when Government bank examinations were inaugurated. I was once told by an old gentleman, one of the early bank examiners, that on one occasion he went into a small-town Iowa bank owned by two brothers. He was allowed to proceed with his work, though he sensed a distinctly hostile attitude. On his next visit he managed to get on a more human basis with the brothers, and at parting the elder brother confided:

"I guess, Mr. Butler, you thought we weren't very friendly the first time you came. Well, we weren't. We thought you might be trying to work some kind of a burglary dodge. All the time you were fussing around the bank my brother and I were watching you, each with a gun in hand. We had agreed that if you made one false move, we were going to shoot."

There is no record of a Dun or a Bradstreet reporter being covered by two guns while interviewing a business firm, yet there was enough drama and adventure in the work of some early reporters to satisfy the most romance-minded person. Colorado in the eighties and nineties of the last century experienced a tremendous boom. Traders flocked in from all parts of the country, many of dubious character, started in business, and sought credit from eastern wholesale concerns. The work of the credit reporter was extraordinarily difficult and loaded with responsibility. In the files at the present Dun and Bradstreet New York headquarters there is preserved a memorandum written by a reporter connected with the old R. G. Dun and Company Denver office:

> Shooting scrapes in a gambling joint next to our office were regular occurrences. Prosperous towns like Leadville and Cripple Creek sprang up overnight, huge bodies of ore were discovered and immense wealth was located in a few months. Men would walk down the main street of the city of Leadville swinging their revolvers by a chain attached to their wrists, ready for use on the slightest provocation. During the entire period we always had traveling reporters to cover the territory. Most of the traveling had to be done on horseback or by stagecoach through the ranches and hills and mining towns infested by desperadoes, half-breeds, cow punchers and tough characters of all kinds. Stage robberies were frequent and the rights of property were often decided by the fitful laws of chance or by the quickness on the trigger.

There still exist romantic and dramatic opportunities in the credit reporter's work. A reporter who recently revised the credit reports on all businesses in Alaska, mostly by direct, personal interviews, covered more than three thousand miles in three months by steamer, railway coach, caboose, and airplane. Credit terms extended to interior Alaska storekeepers are much the same as in our Colonial days, namely, twelve months. Purchases are made largely from Seattle or Tacoma wholesale houses and settlement of accounts is expected upon opening of transportation in the spring, generally payable with the proceeds from the sale of furs.

Northwest Canada is also a difficult country to cover. The opening of new mines has created many boom towns, all of which must be visited. In 1940 a Dun and Bradstreet reporter arrived by airplane at Yellow Knife, Alberta, where three years before there had been only a few Indian shacks and trappers' cabins. When the reporter completed his work he had information on twenty-three concerns that were seeking credit from distant merchandise suppliers.

In 1921 San Antonio, Texas, underwent a disastrous flood from the little river that winds through the city and that ordinarily is barely three feet deep; on that occasion the stream rose between nightfall and dawn to forty feet above normal. Practically the entire retail district was flooded, water rising to the second floors of store buildings, hotels, and wholesalers' warehouses. It was late September and the majority of merchants had received their fall stocks. In many cases the rushing water burst through store fronts and gushed out the rear, carrying off the entire stock of merchandise.

Before the water subsided, credit reporters of both Dun's and Bradstreet's local offices were on the scene, later reinforced by reporters from other

Texas cities. In less than three days every business enterprise within the flooded district had been visited and estimates made regarding the amount of damage in each case.

The work done by these credit reporters and the estimates of losses they sent in to their home offices, turned out to the benefit of business men who had suffered losses. In many cases eastern creditors put off payment dates to give their customers time to recuperate. Some manufacturers sent merchandise, without charge, to replace that which had been destroyed.

When the Pittsburgh district had its disastrous flood in the Spring of 1936, credit reporters were on the ground to make a rapid survey. Each day they sloshed through the mud-covered streets of the Golden Triangle of Pittsburgh, examining premises and interviewing merchants. At night they returned to cold, oil-lighted offices where credit reports were typed, duplicated by the thousands and sent to manufacturers and wholesalers all over the country who had made inquiries. In squads of four, reporters patrolled the populous valleys of the western Pennsylvania district, using automobiles wherever possible. The final check-up showed that more than three thousand concerns in Pittsburgh, Johnstown, and Wheeling had suffered damage, many of the smaller ones requiring credit extension on merchandise bills and additional credit for new fixtures and property repairs.

The same scenes were enacted two years later in Providence, Rhode Island, when a 100-mile-an-hour gale from the South drove the unusually high tide into the heart of the city, causing heavy loss of life and property. Next day credit reporters went to work; within a week every business enterprise had been visited and estimates obtained regarding the amount of damages.

Credit reporting as developed by Dun and Bradstreet, Inc., is a highly specialized profession. Not only is a reporter trained to write and analyze information that business men submit. He learns the ins and outs of different trades; what are the customary credit terms; what turnover is required and what margin of profit on sales is necessary to maintain a healthy business condition; what merchants in different lines may safely owe to suppliers in proportion to their capital. A good reporter acquires a sort of sixth sense that enables him to evaluate credit risks from bits of evidence that might easily escape the ordinary observer. A merchant who accepts the presidency of his chamber of commerce when his business should have his whole attention; a wholesale business started in a high rent section, a retired farmer who invests in a grocery business, a man of hail-fellow manners who opens a drug-store in a select residential neighborhood and allows it to be a loafing place for cronies—all these are straws in the wind that the reporter recognizes as significant and that are to be reflected in his reports.

In one recent case a reporter visited a curio store in a resort city, the owner being a man of foreign extraction. The curio merchant exhibited a carefully prepared statement that showed his stock to be worth about $20,000, with debts about $6,000, a condition that should ordinarily entitle him to a fair credit rating. But the reporter knew something of values in the curio line and was inclined to doubt the $20,000 inventory. Questioning revealed that the merchant had reached that figure by listing his curios at double the wholesale cost. He stoutly defended his system. "I sell everything for double what it costs me," the merchant said, "so that is what it is worth."

The reporter was sophisticated enough to sense at a glance that the merchant's stock was overvalued; but he is still unable to decide if the curio merchant was trying for a good credit rating, or only ignorant.

Shortly before writing this chapter I chanced to have business with the veteran president of a bank in a small county-seat Kansas town. The old gentleman was not a subscriber to the Dun and Bradstreet service; but a manufacturer in a near-by city, recently retired from business, had given the banker a late copy of the Dun and Bradstreet rating book. The banker told me he was amazed at the accuracy of the reports.

"I've been in banking here for more than fifty years," he said, "and I've watched every business man from the time he started and noticed how he got along. I've loaned most of them money when they were entitled to it, and turned them down when they weren't. When I got that Dun and Bradstreet book I checked over the names of our local business men, and in every single case the rating that was set down against a man coincided exactly with what I would base my decision on if he came to my bank and asked to borrow."

Prior to the Second World War Dun and Bradstreet, Inc. had its own offices, connections or correspondents in practically every part of the world except Soviet Russia and some portions of Asia. At present it maintains 152 offices in the United States and 16 in Canada. Each office has its own staff of trained credit reporters. These men, with 50,000 local correspondents in the United States and 8,000 in Canada, cover every city, town and cross-roads village and provide continuous reports on more than two million separate businesses. An executive in New York, Montreal, Chicago, or San Francisco can obtain comprehensive credit data within a few hours regarding any business no matter where located.

During its one hundred years of existence, and under its different appellations, this great organization has played an important part in America's remarkable development. It has made possible the wider use of credit. Barriers of time and distance have been broken down. Commerce is on a surer basis.

· CHAPTER IX ·

How to Make a Failure

IN THE United States, one business out of five goes out of existence every year. There is a complete turnover every five years. In actual bankruptcies, we have nearly double those of peace-time France and Great Britain combined. It is not a record to be proud of, but there it is.

It does not follow that American business men are less intelligent than French or British business men. The explanation, rather, lies in the fact that our country is still in a state of development, while Europe is more or less static. There, nearly every line of business is so crowded that a man's only chance is to buy out an established concern. To start a new business would be only to court disaster.

Even in the professions this holds true. Few young physicians or lawyers hang out their shingles and start from scratch. They "buy" the practices of retiring physicians or lawyers.

But in the United States a man may start a new enterprise with a fair chance of success if he chooses his location wisely, has a reasonable amount of capital and a working knowledge of the business. It is, in fact, the comparative ease with which success comes in our country, that mainly causes our great number of bankruptcies. Every year thousands of men, attracted by the successes they see around them, go into business, often without sufficient experience or capital, and after a time sink into bankruptcy.

No two failures are ever precisely alike, any more than two persons are precisely alike. There may be general points of resemblance; but back of every business mishap are the individual idiosyncrasies of some man or group of men.

A good credit man must be enough of a psychologist to go behind facts and figures and appraise the personal qualities of a man who asks for credit. Quite often a man has some apparently harmless idiosyncrasy that may undermine whatever solid talents he may possess.

An overly conceited man, for example, is not as good a credit risk as a modest man. A conceited man is liable to let his desire to shine in the public eye influence his business judgment. When you drive through the country and in some town see a large building on Main Street that is obviously too elaborate for the community to support, with half the offices vacant, you can be reasonably sure the building was put up to satisfy the ego of the owner rather than to earn dividends on the investment.

Recently I had occasion to visit a medium-sized southern city where there is a rather sad case of that sort. The man was the most successful merchant in the community, rated in the credit agencies at better than $500,000. Many people were always telling him he was a wonderful business man; and, being susceptible to flattery, he got to the point where he believed it himself. He decided to put up a building that would be a monument to his career. It was an eighteen-story building with offices on the upper floors and the merchant's store on the ground floor. He made a trip to New York with the architect to buy elaborate electric-light fixtures and to pass on designs for elevator doors. The merchant had his name in electric lights at the top of his building.

The merchant figured on a two-way profit. He would get a great deal of admiration for being the owner of such a structure. He also figured that the office rentals would pay enough profit so he would get his store rent free. But things turned out the other way. He never could rent enough office space to pay upkeep on the building and interest on the mortgage. The building was really too big for the town. The merchant had to make up the deficit from the profits of his store, and the store couldn't stand it. A bank now owns the building, and the merchant's creditors are running his store. He is out altogether. Almost worse than that, the merchant didn't get any flattery out of his project. People call the building So-and-So's Folly.

The trouble is that when a man builds a monument to his career he generally goes out of his regular line. Just because a man is a wonderful manufacturer or merchant, it doesn't follow that he knows the real-estate business. And a big building is really a real-estate proposition.

Just a few years ago business circles in a large eastern city were shocked when a fifty-year-old manufacturing plant was taken over by a competitor. The business had got into such desperate straits financially that the competitor merely agreed to pay off the debts and the business was thrown in for nothing.

The founder of the manufacturing plant was a well meaning man who, when he retired a dozen years ago, gave the whole thing to his employees. He appointed three major executives, who had been with him a long time, as managers of the business. But the founder fell short in appraising the temperaments of his executives. They were first-class men as employees, but ill suited to be in supreme command. As time went on the tendency of each man was to settle down in a comfortable groove and do things in the grand manner. The business paid dividends a few years, carried on by its own momentum, then gradually went down hill.

The technic of the man who acted as treasurer will give an idea of the manner in which the business was run. When the president of the competing plant went to look over the business, he noticed a limousine in charge of a liveried chauffeur standing at the side of the main office building. He asked the chauffeur if it was a company car. "It's for the treasurer's use," the chauffeur replied. "I drive him to the bank every day. Sometimes twice a day." The president asked if the car was used for anything beside carrying the treasurer to the bank. The chauffeur said it was not. "The treasurer has his own private car and chauffeur to bring him from his home in the morning and take him home in the afternoon."

The tendency to do things in the grand manner extended to less important workers in the corporation. In the basement of the corporation's office building there was an elderly man sitting in a rocking chair with his feet in another chair. When questioned as to his duties, the man said he was a carpenter by profession and acted as assistant to the corporation's general office manager. "Every once in a while," the man said, " a drawer in some one's desk sticks, or a window won't open; then they telephone down to me and I go up and fix it."

The corporation's main manufacturing plant was in a village some thirty miles from the city. There, a mild old gentleman sat in a little cubbyhole of an office whose title was that of assistant sales director. He recorded the orders that came into the plant each day, the exact time that each order was received, and when the order was shipped out. Every night he walked to the railway station to put his reports on the mail car of the train that went through to the city at ten o'clock, so the reports would be in the corporation's office next morning. He had done that for years. But it turned out that nothing was done with these reports. They were merely stacked away, unopened, in an empty storeroom. The general sales manager, who was one of the three executives appointed to run the corporation's affairs, felt it beneath his dignity to bother with small details.

There is another case where a prosperous business fell into bankruptcy because of one man's desire to express his ego. It was a manufacturing concern, with its plant in an industrial town about seventy miles outside of New York City, and in normal times employed seventy or eighty people.

The president of the concern, who also owned a majority of the stock, was a remarkably successful salesman and had customers among the largest buyers in the country. He had to sell at a close margin to the large buyers, but still he made a living profit. But, like most successful salesmen, the president wasn't a good detail man. The factory routine bored him. What he liked better than anything else was the thrill incidental to putting over big sales deals.

Eventually he moved the sales department to New York so as to be in the midst of things and to meet more buyers personally. After that he spent most of his time at the sales office and came to the plant only occasionally. With no one in authority at the plant it was natural that production costs should go up. Costs went up, in fact, until there was no profit at all in the sales the president was making to his big customers. That was what swamped the business.

Perhaps it seems far-fetched to say it was the president's personal vanity that bankrupted his business. But vanity has many ways of expressing itself. The president was vain of his skill as a salesman. He liked to show how much better he was than his competitors in putting over big deals, and was willing to sacrifice other things to get the thrill of superiority. In a different way he was like the merchant I described earlier in this chapter who put up an eighteen-story building to show what a remarkable merchant he was.

I do not wish to give the impression that personal vanity is an altogether bad quality. Without it, the world would not move very fast. Vanity is no more than legitimate ambition when used moderately. It is bad only when it runs away with a man's judgment.

There was a merchant whom I will call Mr. Jones in the city where I was formerly in business. For a number of years he had a store on a side street, where he paid $60 a month rent. He started on $2,000 capital, but it was enough to make out with, because his only employee was a $6-a-week boy, and Mrs. Jones came down to the store to help out during busy times. Eventually he accumulated a stock worth about $18,000, practically all paid for. Though he didn't have any surplus, he discounted his bills and had a good credit rating. He employed four clerks regularly, and took on others at the holiday season.

Eventually Mr. Jones became dissatisfied with his location. Different friends of his attributed it to different reasons. One said salesmen of wholesale houses flattered him into thinking he ought to move.

A salesman, intent on selling a bill, would explain, "Mr. Jones, a merchant as good as you are doesn't belong on a side street!" Another friend said Mr. Jones had an ambition to be president of the Chamber of Commerce, and was afraid they wouldn't elect a side-street storekeeper. Still another friend said Mr. Jones' wife was at the bottom of it. After he became fairly prosperous, Mrs. Jones quit helping out at the store, and got to going in society. She had an inferiority complex on account of working in the store, and thought people would forget about it if her husband moved to a higher-class location.

Anyhow, Mr. Jones moved to Main Street. He paid $450 a month rent there and spent $3,500 on new fixtures. To meet Main Street competition he had to more than double his stock. He went into debt for $20,000 worth of merchandise. He employed twice as many clerks as at the old place. He lasted just under two years.

There was another case of vanity, still more astonishing, in our city. An Italian meat cutter worked several years in a local butcher shop and managed to save $600. He took his capital and started a butcher shop of his own. I dropped in to wish Tony good luck on his opening day and the first thing I noticed was a magnificent cash register, bigger than his chopping block, all gilt and mahogany, and Tony's name in nickel letters. Tony was so excited over it that he could scarcely keep his eyes off it long enough to wait on customers. He was a business man about six weeks. After he was closed up, the local credit agency manager told me that Tony had only $200 out of his $600 to run his business on. He had paid $400 for his grand cash register.

The desire to shine takes any number of different forms. One rather common form is that of a man who fancies himself as a Shrewd Buyer. Any experienced traveling salesman who chances to read these lines will, I am sure, recognize the type. Quite often the Shrewd Buyer is a small-town dealer who wants to prove that no city slicker can put anything over on *him*. He is fond of boasting to friends and business acquaintances, "I never buy any line straight through. I pick out the bargains and leave the rest to the Dumb Dora buyers."

The Shrewd Buyer generally affects a supercilious attitude when he looks over a line of samples. He picks up an article and demands of the salesman, "How much a gross?" He has no idea of buying in gross lots, but thinks by getting the gross price he can get the same figure on a purchase of two dozen. When the salesman names the price the Shrewd Buyer shrugs his shoulders disdainfully and drops the sample as though it burns his fingers.

When the Shrewd Buyer finishes looking over the

line of samples he has generally turned down so many items that his purchases amount only to a few dollars. I once knew a dealer in Lawrence, Kansas, who was called on by a New York manufacturer. Before agreeing to go up to the hotel to look at the manufacturer's line, the Shrewd Buyer said he must have certain concessions on whatever he might purchase. Instead of sixty days dating he must have ninety days, with a cash discount at that time. The cash discount must be 6 per cent instead of the customary 5 per cent. And the manufacturer would have to pay the freight as far as the Mississippi River. The manufacturer finally agreed to these terms and the dealer bought a bill that amounted to exactly $17.50.

The main trouble with the Shrewd Buyer's policy is that he buys so many bills from so many different sources that he gets tangled up in a maze of small debts. If something happens to cause a spell of dull business—a drought in his section, or a slump in farm prices—the Shrewd Buyer may have trouble in meeting the bills as they fall due.

I know of one retail merchant who owed less than $10,000 when he failed, but it was scattered among seventy different firms, in amounts ranging from $150 down to $8.85. The lawyer who handled the case told me the merchant needn't have failed at all if he had confined his buying to half a dozen strong firms that could afford to carry him through a spell of dull business. As it was, no one firm was enough interested in the merchant to care whether he stayed in business or not.

There is one source of failure more closely connected with the desire to shine in the world than most people imagine. I was talking with the credit manager of a Chicago wholesale house about a merchant who had gone bankrupt. The credit manager said, "That man failed because he was such a good civic worker."

Perhaps that needs a little explanation. I happened to know the man the credit manager alluded to. He used to have a sizable farm implement business in a town of some 20,000 population in a western state that I have occasion to visit frequently. Like so many other places the town is full of civic organizations. There is the Senior Chamber of Commerce, the Junior Chamber of Commerce, the Retail Merchants' Association, the City Club, Rotary International, Kiwanis, Lions, and others.

The farm-implement man became a joiner. At first he confined his activities to the Senior Chamber of Commerce; he took his membership seriously and was occasionally appointed on a committee to solicit subscriptions to the Community Chest or to the Spring Carnival. He probably felt he owed this to the community that gave him his living. Doubtless he also felt it didn't do his business any harm to mix with the live wires and to get his name in the newspaper now and then.

Eventually the implement dealer became publicity-conscious. He became a member of other civic organizations, partly to help his business and partly because he liked to be regarded as a leading citizen. He joined the Salesmanship Group, the Altruists, the Advertising Club, and several secret orders. He went to a club luncheon almost every day and stayed away from his business a couple of hours. Often he made speeches that were quoted in the local newspaper. Once he even spoke over the radio and the Chamber of Commerce had his speech printed in pamphlet form and mailed copies all over the state.

Occasionally, when he got back to his implement store, his clerks said some farmer customer had been in to see about a new tractor or a manure spreader, but went out again because the dealer wasn't there to wait on him in person. That worried him a little but he persuaded himself that the farmer would come back later. And even if that didn't happen he figured the free advertising he was getting would be good for his business in the long run.

But that was wishful thinking. A fundamental of advertising is that advertising doesn't pay unless the advertiser is fully prepared to take care of the business his advertising brings in. The implement dealer didn't take care of his business. Sales fell off to such an extent that he got behind in payments to manufacturers. He had a note at the First National Bank that he asked to have renewed two or three times. It was the bank, in fact, that finally caused his downfall. The bank president owned a large farm and was in the market for a tractor. He came to the implement dealer's place several times, only to find the dealer out making a speech somewhere. Finally he bought his tractor elsewhere. The banker decided the dealer was no longer a good risk and sent him word that he would have to pay his note at the bank. The dealer couldn't do that. Other creditors put in their claims and his business was closed up. The last I heard of the implement dealer he was helping his wife run a boarding-house.

· CHAPTER X ·

Credit Man Extraordinary

THERE SEEMS to be more misunderstanding about the credit profession than about any other profession. A great many people have an idea that a credit man is a morose individual, probably with a full beard, who sits in a private office day after day and turns the cold shoulder to business men who want to purchase goods on time; or, when he is not doing that, he writes sharp letters to customers stating that their accounts are past due and same will be turned over to an attorney for collection unless check is received by 10th inst.

There may be credit men of that sort, but if so I have never met one, though it has been my fortune to know rather intimately many credit men in different parts of the United States. Some of these men, in fact, are first-rate business-getters for their firms.

Not long ago I called at the headquarters of a big wholesale house in lower New York City. I knew the credit man, whose name is something like Marshall. Doubtless Mr. Marshall has a private office, but at the time he was sitting at a desk right out in the middle of a busy sales-room, talking with a man who was evidently a small-town merchant. The man wore a suit that didn't fit very well, and he sat uneasily in a chair with his big felt hat squeezed between his legs.

Mr. Marshall rates as one of the best credit men in New York. He has methods all his own in deciding to whom to extend credit. He doesn't go much on stereotyped reports, or even on an applicant's financial worth. He prefers to sit down and chat informally with a would-be buyer, and makes up his mind from the man's conversation rather than from financial figures.

Apparently the credit man was pursuing his favorite tactics on Mr. Greer of South Carolina. That gentleman very likely did not know he was being interviewed from a credit standpoint. Several times I saw him reach into his inside pocket and start to pull out some sheets of paper, but each time the credit man waved the papers back into his visitor's pocket and went on talking about subjects far removed from business.

"Never mind the figures now," he would say. "We'll go out to lunch after a while and then you can show them to me."

It did seem a rather odd way for a credit man to work, right out in the middle of a sales-room where every one could hear the conversation, instead of making it a secret session behind closed doors. I heard Mr. Marshall ask the man from South Carolina what he thought about the price of cotton, how he liked New York, and what team he thought would win the Southern League pennant. Then the conversation got around to automobiles. I saw the credit man lean forward smilingly to ask another question.

"Did you trade in your old car for a new one this year?" he said interestedly.

The man from South Carolina appeared a little embarrassed as he answered, shifting one foot over the other uneasily.

"Well, to tell the truth," he confessed, "I haven't got any car at all. I used to have one, but I sold it two years ago when I went into business. I had to buy a lot of goods on credit and I figured that I didn't have any right to have a pleasure car so long as I owed money to people."

That was about all I heard of the conversation.

A little later I saw the pair go out to lunch together, already friends. I asked the department head with whom I was transacting my own business if Mr. Marshall was attending to professional duties, or merely entertaining a friend from the country. The department head laughed.

"Marshall is a wonderful credit man," he answered. "Out of more than $8,000,000 worth of business last year we had credit losses of less than $2,000.

"Did you notice how he sat with that fellow right in the middle of the sales-room and talked?" he continued. "That is part of his game. When he gets back from taking the merchant to lunch he will come around to each of us and ask what kind of an impression we had of the merchant. In the end he backs his own judgment, but he is influenced by what we say."

The department head laughed again. "You heard Marshall ask the man if he had swapped his old car for a new model. That is Marshall's test question. Some time or other during every interview he invariably puts that question to the man who is applying for credit."

Later on I heard the story of Mr. Greer of South Carolina, and how he had come out in his dealings with Mr. Marshall, the credit man. Greer had come to New York to try to get himself out of a bad situation he was in. His interview with the credit man spelled success or failure for his business.

In Greer's town, like so many small southern places, the business was dominated by one big retail store that carried everything from plows to shoe laces and from men's overalls to ladies' ready-to-wear dresses. The store's big building occupies nearly all one side of the town square; its owners have a controlling interest in the bank, the hotel, and the leading garage. The big store has always been a social center, too. Country families made it their headquarters when in town, debarking there when they arrived in town and mobilizing there when ready to make the trip home.

Greer, it seemed, had worked in the big store, starting when he was fifteen and continuing for nearly twenty years. Before he was thirty he became manager at a salary of $200 a month, which was more than any one else in town earned except the cashier of the bank. He owned his own home and had money out at interest; he had a car, and on Sunday afternoons drove his wife and two children around the country along with other substantial citizens.

Greer tried to buy an interest in the big store, but the stock paid better than 10 per cent in dividends, and none of the owners would part with any of their holdings. Greer and his wife figured things over and finally came to the conclusion that he would start in business for himself.

When Greer told his firm what he had decided to do they offered to let him buy an interest, but it was too late. He had already rented quarters on the other side of the square and made his plans for opening up. He had called his money in that was out at interest, and even sold his car so as to have that much extra money to put into the business.

Greer confided to Mr. Marshall, the credit man, that he had a bit of an argument with his wife when he told her he intended to sell the car, but he felt he must be firm. He said depreciation and upkeep of a good car like theirs cost at least $40 a month, and so long as he would have to owe a good deal of money for merchandise, he had no business to have this expense. The $40 a month would belong to the people who let him have goods on credit.

Greer had about $7,000 to start business with. In order to make a showing against the big store across the square he had to carry a stock of about $20,000. This would be a heavy load, but he felt he could manage it, as there was plenty of business in the community to support two good concerns. If he could get ahead $3,000 or $4,000 a year it wouldn't be long before his assets would catch up with his debts.

He made arrangements with a New York wholesaler to carry him on long credit for an open account of $10,000 on his promise to buy their lines straight through; whatever they did not handle he bought from other concerns on regular terms. In this way he arranged to finance his $13,000 debt. It would have worked out first-rate except that business was too good.

Greer did a good trade right from the start. He knew every one in the community, and then there was the usual number of customers who always come to a new merchant because they imagine they haven't been treated well at the old established stores. But Greer made one mistake in his figuring. Business was done largely on credit. He had to let his goods go out all spring and summer, and wait until late fall for his money when farmers sold their cotton and other crops; and many farmers had an unpleasant habit of holding their crops until Christmas or later, in the hope of getting higher prices. Sometimes the farmers made money by holding their crops, and sometimes they lost. But meanwhile Greer had very little money to send his creditors. His capital was all on his books.

Of course, Greer, being born and bred in the

community, knew how conditions would be, and he had not looked for any great embarrassment from it. When the old firm needed cash to carry its accounts it merely sent its ledger over to the bank and showed the cashier how much money it had outstanding in farmers' accounts. The bank would always advance three-quarters of the amount on the ledger; sometimes more.

When Greer had nearly $10,000 on his books he felt he ought to borrow some money on it, so he carried his ledger over to the bank and told the cashier he would like a loan of a few thousand with the accounts as security.

But the cashier did not take to the idea. He pointed out that accounts against farmers are at best slow assets, and a bank must have its affairs well in hand at all times. Greer told him the bank had always done it for the old concern but the cashier only smiled and said the old concern was a customer of long standing and, of course, must be taken care of.

Then for the first time Greer remembered that the stockholders in the old concern were the same men who controlled the policy of the bank. It was not in human nature that they should go out of the way to forward the fortunes of a competitor. But that didn't help matters any; it was the only bank in town. Greer tried to make banking connections in another town, but the cashier there told him truly that it was his first duty to take care of local merchants and business men.

That put Greer in a fix, and no mistake. His stock was badly run down and needed replenishing. He wrote to the wholesalers who had extended him credit on his opening bill, explaining matters and asking them to ship him goods enough to fill the holes in his stock. Their reply seemed to put the finishing touch on Greer's misfortunes. They wrote they did not feel like increasing his line of credit at the time; they had gone very carefully over the financial statement he sent them and it did not seem to warrant their shipping him any more goods until his present indebtedness should be cut down. The letter ended by saying they would not press for immediate payment of the money already due, but they must positively hold him to the line of credit originally agreed upon.

The fact that they weren't going to sue him right away for his past-due account didn't help Greer a great deal. His stock was run down to such an extent that he lost business all the time; people would come to his store all set to buy from him, and when they found he didn't have what they wanted, would march straight across the square to trade with his big competitor. It would be months before he could hope to get in much of the money he had outstanding on his books. The chances were that by the time he had collected his money he wouldn't have any store.

In this crisis Greer got on the train and came to New York. He had never been there before; he bought his opening bills from traveling salesmen. He went first to the wholesalers who had staked him to the $10,000 credit, thinking a personal interview might accomplish what he had failed to do by writing letters. The credit man was very polite, but very firm. He said he was sorry Greer's affairs were in such a fix, but really he didn't see what he could do about it. He took steps to protect his firm's interest by having Greer sign some notes, payable in the fall when farmers would begin to sell their crops and start settling their bills.

For two days after this interview Greer walked around the streets of New York wondering what he could do. He had never been in a city larger than Atlanta before, and New York seemed mighty hard and impersonal. He looked up at the buildings in the wholesale district, which bore the names of great firms whose names he had seen in the trade papers. It seemed too presumptuous for him to go up to any of them and ask for credit for his little one-horse business down in South Carolina.

At last he worked his courage up to call on the firm where Marshall was credit man. He had never done any business with the firm, but its traveling man had called on him a couple of times, and he thought it might be a bit of an opening wedge if he should go in and mention the traveling man's name. He had just done that when I first saw him facing Mr. Marshall across the desk in the middle of the big sales-room.

He was a little afraid of the credit man at first. The New Yorker was such a polished individual, his clothes perfectly pressed, his finger nails manicured and a slender gold watch chain strung across his upper vest pockets. He appeared as though all his fifty years had been spent in the atmosphere of big business, fashionable hotels, and week-end parties at rich people's houses.

Greer was especially embarrassed when Mr. Marshall asked him the question about trading in his old car for a late model. He told a friend later on that he was afraid it might lower him in the big man's estimation if he confessed he was such a piker that he didn't run a car at all. For a moment he was tempted to say he had just sold the old car because it was too small and was about to buy a larger one. But he took the more straightforward path and confessed the humiliating truth.

When the two men went out to lunch Greer learned that the credit man was not the pampered child of fortune he imagined. Mr. Marshall told him that he, too, clerked in a country store when he first went to work—in Ohio somewhere. He knew a surprising lot about small business. He asked Greer how much store rent he paid, what wages a good clerk got in South Carolina, and what percentage of a week's business was done on Saturday.

Almost before he knew it Greer was talking to the big man with no more embarrassment than he would have felt in conversation with some neighbor back home. He told how he himself opened up the store every morning at half-past six and swept out, then went home to breakfast after the clerks came at half-past seven. He confessed that he didn't even keep a bookkeeper, because he and his wife could do that work in an hour's time every evening.

Mr. Marshall told Greer he wouldn't give a definite reply to his request for credit just then. He suggested that Greer come to the wholesale house next morning about eleven. Presumably Greer wasn't entirely happy the rest of that afternoon and night. Doubtless the thought came to him that he might have made a better impression if he had talked big and let the credit man believe he was an important man in his community instead of telling about the petty economies he practised.

He still appeared uneasy when he went into the

wholesale house next morning. Mr. Marshall took him into his private office and handed him a cigar and asked if he had a good night's sleep. Then he said pleasantly, "Mr. Greer, I guess we can do business with you. I've set you down for all necessary requirements. From what you told me, I judge your most pressing need is enough merchandise to fill the holes in your stock. The sooner it's done the better. I'll turn you over to one of our salesmen and you can start buying right away. Probably you can finish in time to take the night train for home. We'll see that your merchandise goes out to you promptly."

It was more than a year later that I lunched with Mr. Marshall at an uptown hotel. In the course of conversation I mentioned the Greer incident. "How was it," I joked, "that you gave him a line of credit so easily? Did he work on your feelings by crying on your shoulder?"

"He didn't have to do that," Marshall answered. "I put him on our books because we are glad to have him for a customer."

He added with a bit of asperity, "I guess I'm not overburdened with sentiment. I can say 'No!' as well as any one else. Only last week I overheard one of our salesmen say he could do 20 per cent more business on his territory if I weren't such a tightwad on credits."

I told Marshall the salesman's remark wasn't exactly an original one. I had heard a hundred salesmen on the road say it about their credit executives.

Marshall reverted to the Greer incident: "I didn't take snap judgment on him. I couldn't have done a more thorough job if I had spent a month on it. From his talk I found he was willing to work and that he took his obligations seriously. That remark of his about not keeping an automobile because he felt the money belonged to his creditors was a clincher! Before I took him out to lunch I had two or three men in the office speak with him and they were all well impressed. Then right after lunch I telegraphed the National Credit Agency representative in his county for a report. Early next morning I got a reply that corroborated what Greer had told me. So when Greer came to see me at eleven o'clock there was nothing to do but tell him to go ahead and buy his merchandise."

I asked how Greer seemed to be getting on. Marshall said he was doing all right: "One of these days Greer is going to get all his debts paid and then he'll be a valuable customer for us. He still owes us money, but right now I wouldn't sell his account for a hundred cents on the dollar."

· CHAPTER XI ·

Instalment Credit

IN THE year 1698 John Law, a Scotsman living in London, engaged in a duel and had the misfortune to kill his opponent. To escape prosecution he fled to Paris. Law was then twenty-seven years of age, highly educated, already possessing a reputation as a financier, but with a passion for games of chance. From France, Law went to Holland where he made a further study of finance in the bank of Amsterdam. On the death of Louis XIV in 1715, he returned to Paris with a fortune said to amount to $500,000, made by gambling. Securing the patronage of the Duke of Orleans, he promoted a scheme to rehabilitate French financial affairs.

Law believed that "credit was everything," and

that a state might with safety treat possible future profits as the basis of a paper currency. On his promise to loan the King 1,600,000 livres at 3 per cent, he was permitted to organize the Mississippi or West India Company to colonize and draw profit from French possessions in North America. Later this company merged with the French East India Company under the title of "Company of the Indies." It extended its capital to 624,000 shares, each share valued at 550 livres. An extraordinary fever of stock gambling was excited by these financial manipulations, and shares were eagerly bought by the public at prices that rose to 30 or 40 times the original price.

Law was appointed controller general of the finances. He constantly made huge issues of government notes, with no backing other than the profits his company was expected to earn. By 1720 these notes amounted to nearly 2,000,000,000 livres. The inevitable crash came and Law fled the country. Apparently he was honest and sincerely believed in his scheme. It is said he carried only 800 livres with him when he fled the country. He died in great poverty in Venice.

It seems to be a curious quirk of human nature that periodically some scheme for mortgaging the future, not radically different from John Law's scheme, gains enormous popularity. The latest exhibition in our own country took place during the nineteen twenties. The philosophy was the same as Law's: "Credit is everything." Specifically, it was instalment credit that was counted on to produce lasting prosperity.

Up to about 1921, business in the United States was carried on with reasonable conservatism. There was little "high pressure" selling. Instalment sales were confined mainly to cheaper grades of household furniture, sewing-machines and similar lines. There was a feeling among first-class people that to buy on instalments was not quite dignified. A person of social standing either paid cash, or had the purchase charged to his regular account.

Even automobile sales were conducted in that manner. On one occasion a convention of automobile manufacturers was held in New York and the proceedings were reported in trade journals. The manufacturers expressed themselves strongly against time-payment sales. Mr. Leland, Cadillac general manager, said, "This company has no intention of ever considering the matter of selling automobiles on instalments." A Reo executive stated, "The man who hasn't the money to pay for a machine has no right to own one."

The change from a cash economy to a time-payment economy was brought about through a situation similar to that which existed in France two hundred years earlier. "Hard times" gripped the country. During the four years of the First World War business flourished; manufacturing was stepped up to supply demand. It was believed business would continue good for a number of years; but by 1920 it was only too evident that supply had caught up with, and exceeded, demand. There was a huge surplus of goods. Merchants everywhere were overstocked. Business was in a state of chaos. On main streets all over the country goods were offered at ruinous prices, but with few buyers. There was an epidemic of bank and commercial insolvencies.

In this crisis the idea grew that prosperity might be retrieved by extension of credit to the masses. Automobile manufacturers along with producers in other industries adopted the time-payment plan and arranged to finance their dealers for instalment sales.

As in John Law's time, the expedient had a happy beginning. Millions of people formerly denied credit grasped at the opportunity to secure automobiles, talking-machines, wrist-watches, fur coats, electric toasters, merely by paying down a small amount of cash and signing a contract that called for weekly or monthly payments extending over the following year or eighteen months. By

1926, government estimates set the outstanding instalment contracts at more than $3,000,000,000. A little later it had risen to $4,000,000,000. The average instalment debt of every American family amounted to $250.

Business boomed. Everywhere there was a pleasant feeling of security and a belief that even better things were in store. Writers in Sunday supplements affirmed stoutly that at last the Good Life had been attained. Herbert Hoover, then Secretary of Commerce, was quoted as saying that the policy of instalment selling is "the backbone of continuing American prosperity." There was a tendency to encourage instalment transactions by making them appear virtuous. Professor Irving Fisher of Yale University wrote, "The American practice of instalment buying is a distinct aid to thrift."

I recall an astonishing statement made to me in the course of an interview with a high-ranking executive of one of the largest corporations in the country: "Our American factories are turning out goods by mass production. The goods are immediately disposed of through instalment sales. The money goes right back to the manufacturer to produce more goods. It is the nearest thing to perpetual motion that was ever invented!"

It was quite natural that such extreme optimism

should have encouraged the frenzied speculation in bank and industrial stocks that took place during our nineteen twenties, just as optimism encouraged speculation in John Law's time when shares in his company sold for 30 or 40 times their original price and "land near Paris rose to the value of one hundred years' purchase and most objects of commerce in the same proportion." Doubtless our era of stock speculation was still further encouraged by publication of a two-volume book entitled *Recent Economic Changes,* written by a group of business and economic leaders known as the President's Committee. The committee was extremely optimistic. It stated that recent years—those during which instalment selling had become general—were "splendid beyond all human experience." Of the future the committee predicted, "Economically we have a boundless field before us; there are new wants which will make way endlessly for newer wants, as fast as they are satisfied." Full justice was accorded instalment selling: "The use of instalment credit was a means of lessening sales resistance."

It would be useless to recall these matters except for the light they throw on instalment credit and its relation to general prosperity. It may be well, first, to investigate the actual cost of selling goods on terms of so much down and so much per week or month. One thing is certain: *When an industry goes on an instalment basis the cash price tends to rise somewhere near the instalment price.*

To illustrate: I am, let us say, an electrical-goods merchant. Before the Second World War, when there was no inhibition on manufactured goods, one of my profitable lines was that of washing-machines. One popular seller was a machine that I sold on instalments for $100. But an occasional customer came along who did not wish to buy on time payments and so, to get his trade, I put up a sign, "Ten Per Cent Discount for Cash."

When I sold this cash customer a machine for $90 I charged him too much. Had I been fair with him I should have sold the machine at $25 less than the instalment price. Very likely it cost me even more than $25 to sell a machine on instalments when I figured the expense of bookkeeping, the wages of my collector who went around to collect the weekly payments, and the occasional machine that I was obliged to have the sheriff repossess for me when the purchaser did not make his payments. And the machine that I repossessed was no longer new. I had to sell it as a second-hand article.

I knew all these things. But I did not dare to offer a cash buyer more than a 10 per cent discount. If I did, I could not sell my machines to instalment buyers. I had to make them believe they were paying only a little more than the cash price. My advertisement in the local paper, "I trust the Public," would have been flung in my teeth a dozen times a day by indignant would-be instalment purchasers who learned that I trusted them, but charged them 25 per cent for the compliment.

From the government comes corroboration of the situation I have described above. Business journals throughout the country have printed this news item under a Washington date line: "Cash customers should not be burdened by the cost of the instalment system. One government department to-day is receiving complaints of the practice of selling for cash at the same price as for deferred payment; this is considered bad."

At one time an attempt was made to organize the house-paint industry on a time-payment basis. Several leading house-paint manufacturers combined to promote the idea under the slogan, "Good News to Home Owners—Ten Months to Pay." The plan called for the coöperation of hardware merchants throughout the United States. Any householder who wished to redecorate his house could apply to his local hardware merchant, and the latter would supply the paints and arrange with a painting contractor to do the work. When the job was finished the householder paid one-fifth the agreed price in cash and signed ten notes for the balance.

It was, apparently, a splendid arrangement for every one concerned. The householder was charged only 9 per cent above the cash price. Assuming the cash price, for example, to be $300 for painting a house, the householder paid $327 on the instalment plan. The hardware dealer who sold the paint did not have to wait for his money. He sent the householder's ten notes to a finance company. The finance company mailed the hardware dealer a check.

Yet with all its seeming advantages, the plan had to be abandoned because of violent opposition from associations of hardware dealers. Inasmuch as these merchants apparently stood to gain by selling house-painting jobs on the instalment plan, what were their reasons for refusing to coöperate?

The principal reason, as announced by the National Retail Hardware Association, was the excessive price charged the householder. In a letter sent to its members the Association stated: "When great industries compete with each other for larger sales by educating consumers to buy credit at 20 per cent to 30 per cent interest cost, the situation deserves serious thought."

How did the National Retail Hardware Association arrive at its conclusion that interest cost was

"20 per cent to 30 per cent," when the promoters of the Good-News-to-Home-Owners campaign expressly stated that the householder was charged only 9 per cent? The explanation is very simple: The householder who bought a $300 job of house painting on ten months' time did not get $300 worth of credit. He paid $60 as soon as the job was finished. The most he owed, therefore, was $240. He cut this down every month, and at the tenth month he owed only $24. But he had to pay interest on $300 for the entire ten months!

A hardware merchant in Muncie, Indiana, explained the retailer attitude when he wrote his trade journal: "Instalment buying costs the consumer an interest rate of about 25 per cent. The more money he pays for interest the less he has to pay for merchandise."

If the Muncie hardware merchant had gone into the instalment house-painting project, he would have charged his customers $1 for $.75 worth of paint and labor. The other $.25 would have gone out of town to the finance company. The merchant would have reduced the buying power of his own customers. If all the merchants of Muncie had simultaneously begun to vend their wares on instalments, the buying power of every one in Muncie would have been reduced.

One unfortunate feature of instalment operations is the temptation for sellers to juggle with figures in order to conceal the cost of time-payment credit, as did the paint manufacturers in their Good-News-to-Home-Owners campaign. It will be recalled that in the late 1930's the government stepped in to compel the automobile industry to discontinue its practice of advertising a 6 per cent interest charge on time-payment sales. The real interest charge—taking into account the down payment and the steady reduction of the balance due —was between 11 and 12 per cent.

As a matter of fact, an instalment credit sale as generally transacted is not credit at all. It is pawnbroking. If I go into a time-payment store and purchase a second-hand automobile or a radio set, the dealer does not trust me to make my payments. He makes me admit that I am not honest enough to give him back the car or the radio set in case I am unable to pay. He insists that I sign a paper giving him the right to take back my purchase and even to put me in jail if I try to run away with it. The laws in force throughout the country permit the dealer to do that. In all but three states,—Louisiana, Missouri, and Ohio—there is a fiction that the car or the radio set is the property of the dealer until I have made my last payment.

It is true, as the President's Committee wrote, that the use of instalment credit was "a means of lessening sales resistance." Yet it is the people who can least afford it whose sales resistance is most easily lessened. A business investigator reports seeing in a store in Tennessee a piece of household furniture that had been sold on instalments and repossessed from Negro families no less than sixty-seven times. This is known in the trade as "borax" selling. Another example was that of a Mexican day laborer in San Antonio, Texas, who had in his adobe shack a set of dining-room furniture for which he had promised to pay $400. As the Mexican had a wife and several children and earned $1.50 a day, it was evident he had done business with a borax merchant who hoped to collect two or three payments and then seize the merchandise.

An industrial life insurance company reports a case in Rochester, New York, concerning the death of a man who had been regularly earning $60 a week as a high class steam-fitter. He had bought on instalments an automobile, a fur coat for his wife, a handsome radio set, and other articles. The weekly instalments on these purchases amounted to $63. As his budget left nothing for house rent or groceries, he had to miss about half his payments each week, and always there was an unseemly race between instalment collectors to see which should be first to reach the steam-fitter when he came home with his pay envelop. By making payments every second week he had managed to avoid having any purchases seized. When he died his widow received a check for $1,500 from the insurance company; but this left her still some $700 short of the amount necessary to complete her instalment payments. Questioned as to the family's peculiar financial arrangements, she said, "I guess we didn't realize what we were doing. Everywhere we went some one urged us to buy something on the instalment plan and offered to let us have it with such a little down payment that we couldn't resist. They said it was the modern way to save money."

Does the theory that "instalment selling is the backbone of continuing American prosperity" stand up under analysis? Can prosperity be increased by forcing the sale of articles this year that will not be paid for until next year, or the year after? Under any known system of logic, it can not. It is merely a synthetic prosperity until customers have paid off some of their instalments and are once more a safe risk. Prosperity really is undermined, because if customers pay large sums for the privilege of buying on instalments they have just that much less to spend for goods. Mr. James H. Perkins, chairman of the board of the National City Bank of New York, seems to have stated the case clearly when he said to a senatorial committee: "The idea that the way to prosperity is to make it easy for people to get into debt does not stand the test of experience."

It is astonishing, when one thinks of it, how many easy ways there are for people to get into debt. Railroads, and even air lines, have organized to sell travel with a small cash payment and the balance in instalments after the trip has been made. Previous to the Second World War, transatlantic steamship lines, both British and American, offered voyages to Europe at so much down and the balance in instalments after the voyager's return. But it was a one-way arrangement. British lines did not advertise instalment trips to the United States. Apparently British steamship magnates believed it correct to tempt Americans to go into debt for purposes of pleasure, but not for their own people.

Perhaps the most outstanding credit development in our country during recent years is the establishment of personal-loan departments by commercial banks, where credit is sold on instalments. Prior to 1929 there were a mere half-dozen banks that had personal-loan departments. By 1934 the number had grown to seventy-one. Now there are several thousand. One large New York bank with seventy-odd branches in the five boroughs has a record of making more than a thousand loans to men and women each business day. Nine persons out of ten who apply for loans are accommodated. Repayment is required over a period of one year, in monthly instalments.

Doubtless this service is a boon to a great many people. Recently I sat during several hours beside one of the men who interviews applicants for loans in a large New York bank. The majority of applicants wanted money for useful purposes—to pay hospital bills, insurance premiums, taxes, to help relatives. Yet there was an angle to it that might be criticized as being a little short of constructive. The bank is in the personal-loan business to make money; such being the case, it was understandable that little distinction should be made between loans for constructive purposes and those not so constructive. It was illuminating to learn how close many people are sailing to the wind financially, when they might have a margin for eventualities except for the temptations of easy credit. One young married couple, the man earning $80 a week, wanted money for a vacation at a resort hotel. The corporation he works for had set his vacation time two weeks earlier than he expected, and he was caught without the necessary money. A girl stenographer, working for another corporation at $30 a week, also wanted vacation funds. The thought occurred to me that had the young lady spent less on lip rouge and blood-red fingernail paint, she might have been in a position to pay cash for her holiday. Both the girl and the young man were granted loans on the same terms as the individuals who wanted money for hospital bills and for helping unfortunate relatives.

It might seem a bit overly generous that the bank should loan money to nine applicants out of ten. But the generosity is more apparent than real. The moment the applicant leaves the interviewer's desk, other bank employees take up the case. They telephone the firm the applicant claimed he or she works for. How long has the applicant been in the firm's employ? Is his salary what he said it is? Is his work satisfactory? Is his job likely to last? Does he live at the address he stated on his application blank? After that they telephone a central credit clearing house to learn if the applicant owes money at any other bank or personal-loan agency, and if he has ever been sued for debt.

The bank considers carefully the sort of firm the applicant works for. If it is a firm with a reputation for hiring and firing conservatively—for example, the New York Telephone Company or the Edison Electric Company—that is in the applicant's favor. It is not so favorable, however worthy the applicant may be or how desperately he needs money, if he works for an east-side restaurant or some feebly financed textile concern.

And so, instalment sales of credit are not based altogether on the applicant's sterling character, but the character of the firm that employs him. It was not that way in the pre-instalment era. Then a man built up his credit standing gradually and solidly. He became known in his community as a steady, reliable person who looked ahead and tried to save a portion of his income as a reserve for eventualities. If anything happened that required the use of credit, local people stood ready to accommodate him with cash or goods on his plain promise to pay.

Is prosperity really worth while that depends on getting millions of wage earners into debt? Isn't a man undermining his character just a little when he regularly buys things on instalments or finances vacation trips through the bank's personal-loan department, instead of saving up the price in advance? I believe he is. I believe, for example, that the Rochester steam-fitter I have mentioned was a more upstanding citizen in the days before he tangled himself up so heavily in time-payment contracts that collectors raced to his house to see who would be first to reach his pay envelop.

It is rather well established that instalment selling is not a sound basis on which to build permanent prosperity. During the depression that followed the business débâcle of 1929, instalment sales were pushed more intensively than ever. Down payments were reduced and longer time accorded on purchases. In Detroit, instalment merchants used full-page newspaper advertisements that urged the buying of Christmas gifts with no down payment: "The purchaser may begin to pay on February first." Montgomery Ward, the Chicago mail order house, announced that it would sell on instalment articles that cost as little as $10. Formerly the concern's smallest instalment transaction was $20. It was reported in the trade press that some public utility companies were "passing out electric refrigerators costing $200 or $300 for a down payment of only $10." But such frantic bids for sales did not bring back prosperity. The theory that instalment selling is the "backbone of continuing American prosperity," did not work out in practice. The depression of the 1930's was more severe and lasted longer than any other depression in our history.

No one will assert that instalment selling is an unmitigated evil. If the abuses are eliminated it may be beneficial both to industry and the public. The principal abuses are "borax" selling and the high-pressure pushing of goods on people beyond their ability to pay. I might also mention the practice of forcing an instalment purchaser to sign a contract that makes him admit he is not quite honest.

There is a very simple way to avoid these abuses: Eliminate the *contract* that entitles the seller to retain title to an article after he has delivered it to his customer. In certain foreign countries there are laws that expressly forbid such an arrangement. When an article changes hands, the title goes with it. If I, for example, sell a radio set to a person and deliver it to him, the radio set is his, even though he has not paid me anything on it. To be safe, I must assure myself of one of two things: either that my customer is financially responsible for the amount, so I may sue him in the courts and get my money; or, that my customer has such a reputation for honesty that he will bring back my radio set in case he finds himself unable to meet his payments under the law. I may not even pretend that I have rented the radio set to my customer, and so keep the title in my own hands.

Far be it from me to recommend the passing of more laws when we have too many laws already; but such a statute would go far to eliminate dangerous overselling in our country. Credit would be a dignified matter, depending on the purchaser's known reputation for honesty rather than on a threat of sending the sheriff after him. The only persons who might object to such a law would be those who stand to make money by "borax" selling, or by high-pressure pushing of goods on people, beyond their ability to pay.

· CHAPTER XII ·

Banks and Bankers

BANKING IS, perhaps, one of the least understood of human enterprises. I believe it is not an exaggeration to state that scarcely one person out of three who patronizes a bank has more than a vague idea of what actually goes on inside his bank. He knows his bank accepts his money and records the sum in his pass book. When he wishes to draw out money he writes a check. He knows the bank loans money; but in the back of his mind is the idea that it is done grudgingly, and only after the borrower has pledged securities far in excess of the money loaned.

In case any reader has ever mingled in the affairs of some commercial community he will doubtless have heard disgruntled business men, who have applied unsuccessfully for bank accommodation, use the phrase: "There isn't a real banker in this town. They're just a lot of pawnbrokers!"

Then there is the time-worn anecdote of the banker with one glass eye. A would-be borrower, looking anxiously into the banker's face, mistook the glass eye for the normal one and concluded it had the greater element of human sympathy.

All of which is, of course, one hundred per cent fictitious. A banker wishes to loan money just as much as a merchant wishes to sell goods. That is his way of earning a living. If he did not make loans his bank could not exist. But there is one vital difference between merchandising and banking that inclines a good banker to conservatism. The merchant owns the goods that he has for sale. The banker does not own the money he has for loaning purposes. It belongs to his depositors.

One has only to go back a few years to learn what may happen when bankers in large numbers abandon their traditional conservatism and conduct their affairs more in accordance with the desires of ambitious borrowers. From the borrowers' standpoint the years between 1923 and 1929 were ideal. One scarcely needed to ask for credit; in many cases credit was forced on one. In another chapter I describe how bankers went up and down their Main Streets to say to merchant-depositors, "Couldn't you use some extra money to expand your business? If so, come down to the bank!"

Between 1930 and 1933, 27 per cent of all banks in the country suspended operations. More than $5,000,000,000 were tied up in the suspended banks. The country paid heavily for its financial overoptimism.

It requires considerable courage to be a good banker. There must be occasions when even the traditional banker with a glass eye regrets to say "No" to some hard-pressed person seeking a loan. A currently very successful banker of my acquaintance began his career in a bank that was started by a group of well-to-do farmers in a cross-roads Ohio village of less than three hundred population. He was the only regular employee; his salary was $35 a month, for which he swept out, stoked the base-burner stove and acted as bookkeeper, teller, and cashier. The president, a shrewd farmer, spent a part of each day at the institution in an advisory capacity. My friend was twenty-one, and of a conciliatory disposition; he had a habit, when some customer of dubious responsibility applied for a loan, of calling on the president to make the necessary refusal. One day the president took him to task.

"You'll never be a banker," the president said,

"the way you're doing. I don't want you running to me when there's a disagreeable job to do. If you know a man is no good, turn him down yourself!"

A great many men who now are heads of outstanding banks in the big cities of the country served their apprenticeships in just such country towns. There is a quite understandable reason. The man who first goes to work in a great city institution seldom has a chance to learn more than one specialty. He may know that specialty down to his finger tips, but the rest is more or less strange territory to him. But the man who learned his trade in a little town—who ran up and down Main Street to collect notes and drafts, kept books, stood in a teller's cage, perhaps negotiated loans on mules and yearling calves—he had to be somewhat under average intelligence if he did not get a fairly clear idea of what banking is all about.

The first bank that at all corresponds to modern financial institutions, and of which there are fairly reliable data, was established in ancient Greece, where banking seems to have been an important industry. The State Bank of Ilium, established during the second century before the Christian era, accepted deposits from citizens for which it paid 10 per cent interest and made loans to the state. The first bank in medieval times was the Bank of Venice, organized in the twelfth century, when

Venice was "the most splendid city in Europe." Its paper was so highly regarded that for long periods it was at a premium over coins, that were often worn or "clipped." The Bank continued in existence until 1797, when the Venetian Republic was overthrown by the army of Revolutionary France.

Other European banks were established, in Genoa in 1345, and in Barcelona in 1401. The Bank of Amsterdam was founded in 1609, and the Bank of Hamburg in 1619. The Bank of England was founded under the reign of William and Mary in 1694.

These early banks were established primarily to make it possible for governments to borrow money at more reasonable rates than those charged by private lenders. During the William and Mary reign, for example, the war with France made large borrowings necessary; the Government was paying an interest rate of 20 to 40 per cent. The new Bank of England loaned the Government at 8 per cent, plus £4,000 a year for bank expenses.

Before that, in the reign of Henry III, there was set a record for high interest charges scarcely surpassed by present-day loan sharks. The Pope offered Henry the crown of Sicily for his son Edmund, and the king was involved in debt by his endeavors to support the claim. He borrowed in Italy, at an interest rate of 120 per cent per annum, with an additional charge in case payments were not made on due dates.

Apparently money-lenders did not regard kings as first-class credit risks, which may account for the high interest rates. In the reign of Charles I, money-lending was in the hands of London goldsmiths, who deposited their funds at the Royal Mint in the Tower of London. But Charles, being in need of money, seized the money thus deposited, amounting to £200,000. The goldsmiths were again despoiled in 1672, when Charles II followed the example of his father and appropriated their money amounting to £1,328,562, on which there accrued twenty-five years' interest, the total amounting to more than £3,000,000.

There were no banks in America prior to our Revolutionary War. Certain functions of banking were carried on by wealthy merchants in the seacoast cities, who accepted deposits and granted loans to friends and customers. They also sold bills of exchange, which served the purpose of modern letters of credit. Thomas Hancock of Massachusetts was one of these merchant-bankers, as was also Nathaniel L. Savage, who carried on extensive operations in Virginia. Merchants and individual money-lenders eventually discontinued their activities as result of depreciation of continental and state currencies during the Revolutionary War and when, as General George Washington wrote, "a wagon load of money will scarcely purchase a wagon load of provisions."

The Bank of North America, our first commercial bank, was organized in Philadelphia in 1781 by Robert Morris. The enterprise was immediately successful; profits for the first half-year amounted to 4½ per cent, and dividends for 1783 averaged 14 per cent. The Bank of New York was organized in 1784, under articles of incorporation drawn up by Alexander Hamilton. The Massachusetts Bank, in Boston, opened its doors one month after the Bank of New York. There was a bit of typical New England foresight in one of the Massachusetts Bank's rules concerning deposits, as recorded in Roy A. Foulke's excellent book, *The Sinews of American Commerce:**

> Funds received as deposits were the various kinds in common circulation at the time—Portuguese johanneses, Spanish doubloons, British guineas, French Louis d'or and Mexican dollars. Because of the uncertain value of these coins, the Bank enforced the rule that a depositor should be permitted to withdraw only the same kind of money that he had deposited.

It was not until 1791 that the fourth bank in the country was established, the Bank of the United

* Published by Dun and Bradstreet, Inc., 1941.

States, located in Philadelphia. It received its charter from Congress, and the Federal Government took $2,000,000 of its stock, to be paid for in ten equal instalments. This bank issued paper money, that was accepted at par throughout the country; it acted as fiscal agent of the Government by collecting, disbursing, and caring for its funds. The institution was highly profitable, paying more than 8 per cent in dividends, besides gaining a profit of $671,800 on the sale of stock originally purchased by the Government. In a little over ten years these shares had risen from a par value of $400 to $580 per share. So profitable was the institution, in fact, and so high its reputation abroad, that by 1811 a majority of its shares had been acquired by European investors. That may have been a contributing factor for the refusal of Congress to renew its charter, in 1811. When the bank went out of existence, Stephen Girard of Philadelphia, then the richest man in the country, purchased the bank building and equipment and opened his own institution under the name of Stephen Girard's Bank.

Meanwhile the number of commercial banks in the country had increased rapidly. In 1811 there were forty-eight. In 1816, 246; by 1837, the year of the tremendous business collapse, the number had risen to 788.

There are no authoritative figures on the number

of commercial bankruptcies that occurred as a result of the 1837 collapse, but it is known that in New York City alone, in two months, there were more than 250 failures. The percentage of failures in the entire country was probably the greatest in our history, greater, even, than that following our 1929 débâcle. And, as in the latter case, the principal cause was speculation—the desire to get rich quickly without undue labor.

The greatest speculation of the 1830's was centered in public lands, though there was considerable activity in town and city lots. It was a time of tremendous optimism. Merchants bought goods lavishly in anticipation of ever increasing sales. In five years the volume of Anglo-American trade doubled; in the year ending September 30, 1836, our imports from Great Britain exceeded our exports to that country by more than twenty million dollars.

Also, as in the years immediately preceding 1929, speculation was encouraged by local bankers in many cases. Among the 788 banks existing in the country in 1837, a great many were organized by men with little knowledge of banking. These men did not hesitate to persuade business men to borrow:

Local merchants were invited by the organizers and the inexperienced officers of these new banking institutions to borrow funds for enlarging their business operations. The merchants were no more hesitant to accept these offers than men of limited resources from 1927 to 1929, who, in their mad haste to become wealthy, bought country land, city office buildings, merchandise of all kinds, securities on moderate margins, and experienced no great difficulty in obtaining credit to carry on these "profitable" undertakings.*

Apparently the phrase, "If you want some money, come down to the bank," was spoken on Main Streets during the optimistic 1830's quite as often as on Main Streets during the fabulous 1920's. When credit begins to be hawked about like groceries or dry-goods, wise men know it is time to look out for trouble.

Banking practices in the early days differed considerably from those in vogue at the present time. To-day, the principal functions of a commercial bank are to receive deposits and to loan money. The early banks made loans, but the public did not think of banks essentially as places for the deposit of money. Banks were not important as depositories except for government funds.

A business man in the early days who wished to borrow, went to his bank and signed a note. The bank did not, as now, give him credit on its books for the amount of the note, less interest, on which

* Roy A. Foulke, *op. cit.*

he may draw checks from time to time. Instead, the bank handed him actual currency which he took away with him. The modern "checking account" did not come into general use for a great many years. The Bank of New York was first to develop largely the practice of crediting loans to deposits. In 1841 that institution had deposits of more than $1,250,000, subject to check. The Massachusetts Bank in Boston was next to New York in amount of deposits subject to check, slightly over $200,000.

At that time Boston was a city of more than 100,000 population. As an illustration of the growth of bank deposits, it may be mentioned that exactly one hundred years later, in 1941, the town of Eaton, Ohio, an average small community of 3,500 people, had two banks with deposits running well over $3,000,000.

Up to the last quarter of the nineteenth century, it was customary for banks to loan money on "two-name paper": that is, a note signed by the person who wished to borrow the money, and bearing the signature of another person as endorser. The theory was, of course, that the responsibility of two men was twice as good as the responsibility of one man. Yet the practice had its defects, the most serious one being that, to an inexperienced banker, the name of an endorser of a note was likely to give a false sense of security. The banker was inclined not to investigate the responsibility of either signer as closely as he would if only one man were involved.

Some years ago Mr. James B. Forgan, then Chairman of the Board of the First National Bank of Chicago, described in a bulletin of the National Association of Credit Men, the conditions in a town where he obtained some of his early banking experience:

> There were three banks in the town and practically all of their loans were made on notes having two endorsers. A great depression occurred in the principal industry of the locality and considerable liquidation of bank credits became necessary. The banks soon found, however, that the money they had thus loaned had been largely invested in fixed property. The banks in many cases refused to renew the notes and they lay past due. They began to bring pressure on the makers and endorsers alike but soon awoke to the fact that all their borrowing customers were so involved as endorsers for each other that they resembled a row of bricks standing on end so that if one were knocked down it would fall on another until all were laid low.

During the decade that began in 1870, a few banks began to make loans on single-name paper. Though at first it was considered a hazardous experiment, the practice spread; by 1900 single-name paper became the usual basis for loans both in city and in small town banks.

At about the turn of the century, too, another innovation took place—the organization of "Bank Credit Departments." Banks began systematically to collect and analyze facts concerning business firms in their communities, for the guidance of loaning officers.

Years ago, when bank credit departments were all but unknown except in a few large cities, Mr. James B. Forgan made an address in which he stated that "a bureau of credit is a desirable department in every well managed bank, however small," and went on to say it should be the duty of a banker to leave records for those who follow him: "The information on which a bank grants credit is obtained by the banker in his official capacity and is, therefore, the bank's property."

In a small town or village bank, where the majority of bank customers are known personally, the credit department records may be handled by the part-time work of a single employee. In some of the large institutions of the country the full-time work of one hundred or more persons is required.

The credit department builds up credit records on all customers of the bank, both those who borrow and those who do not borrow. In the case of a customer who does not borrow, but who carries a checking account, the department obtains sufficient information to establish his identity and general reputation for integrity. A bank should know something regarding the character of a person who deposits money and writes checks. An individual who has a habit of writing checks without a sufficient balance to cover them is undesirable. The management of a bank dislikes to decline payment of its own checks. Nor for its own reputation does a bank like to accept the accounts of persons of questionable character.

Quite naturally, however, the credit department concerns itself more particularly with customers who are on a borrowing basis with the bank, or customers who may at some future time request accommodation. The bank credit department obtains and files away information gained from the Dun and Bradstreet agency; and, in case the customer is engaged in an industry that has its own credit reporting bureau, such as the Lumberman's Credit Association, Inc., the Jewelers Board of Trade, the Shoe and Leather Mercantile Agency, Inc., etc., information from those sources is often acquired. Also, the credit department makes inquiries at other banking institutions to ascertain their experience with a customer who has done business with one or more banks. The credit department, further, gets information from business houses with which the customer has had dealings, to learn if the dealings have been generally satisfactory; if the customer under investigation has paid his bills promptly; if he has, or has not, made claims often for shortage in invoices, or goods not up to sample; in other words, information to show whether or not the person is a fair trader.

In case a customer brings to the bank a note given him by some concern with which he does business, and asks to have the note discounted (though "cashed" is a more understandable word), the credit department should have a report on the financial status of the concern that executed the note.

In case a customer wishes to borrow a large sum and as security offers to pledge certain assets, such as stocks, bonds, mortgages, or real estate, the credit department must obtain information regarding the actual value of the assets offered as collateral. The department may also recheck the value of the pledged assets from time to time until the loan is liquidated.

Where a business man seeks an "unsecured" loan—that is, a loan on his unsupported promise to pay—the bank requires him to present a balance sheet, a profit and loss statement, and a record of the past performance of his business. In such a case the loan is not "unsecured"; it is based on the business man's present financial worth, plus his proved business ability and his general reputation for integrity. The loan is really backed by the business man's entire assets, both financial and moral.

It is the function of the bank's credit department to have all information ready to place before the loaning officer when that officer is face to face with a would-be borrower and must give a definite Yes or No. The credit department might be likened to the supply division of an army, and the loaning officer to the commander at the front. The efficiency of the loaning officer depends on the efficiency of the credit department.

Suppose we select a few actual incidents from everyday banking experience and see how a banker comes to decisions regarding requests for loans. The names of business men and places are fictitious:

Horace L. Fentiman is proprietor of a trunk and leather goods store in Farless, Texas, a town of some twenty-five thousand population, with a good farming-trade territory. Mr. Fentiman has been in business twenty-six years, coming from Chicago where he learned the trunk-making trade. In his Farless store he makes some inexpensive trunks, working between customers in a room at the back of the store, with the aid of one assistant. He is well known to John Hayes, president of the First National Bank.

For a number of years Mr. Fentiman has made seasonal borrowings; and, in accordance with the wishes of the First National president, has brought in each year a detailed statement of his business. For the year in question the statement was as follows:

ASSETS

Value of merchandise on hand, at wholesale cost	$7,257.85	
Money owing from customers	1,878.50	
Cash on hand and in bank	963.90	
Total Assets		$10,100.25

LIABILITIES

Owing to manufacturers for merchandise	$1,447.63	
Accrued expenses, taxes, electricity, etc.	173.70	
Total Liabilities		$ 1,621.33
Net worth of business (assets less liabilities)		$ 8,478.92

As further assets, Mr. Fentiman owns his store building, that he values at $14,000. But, as he lives with his family in an apartment on the second floor of his building, the property, according to Texas State laws, is classed as a homestead and may not be seized for debts of the owner.

His sales for the year were $27,000, on which he figured there was a net profit of $2,100. About two-thirds of his sales were cash, the balance charged on his books. Average collection period of charges about forty-five days. His store fixtures and shop equipment originally cost about $2,000, but he does not list them as assets because they are somewhat old and would bring next to nothing in case he should close out his business.

When Mr. Fentiman came to the bank, in October, he asked to borrow $2,500 with which to buy merchandise for the forthcoming holiday trade. He wishes to pay cash to the manufacturers in order to earn the cash discounts. He expected to liquidate his bank loan in January.

There was no doubt that Mr. Fentiman was good for the loan he requested. He had worked up to his present position from small beginnings. He was industrious and reliable. His sales were somewhat above average for his line of business. There was but the barest formality in executing the loan. Mr. Fentiman signed a ninety-day note, and the amount was placed to his credit. He was at liberty to draw on it at once.

Below is the record of a business of much larger caliber. The Allison Wholesale Grocer Company, located in the city of Northwest, Ohio, dates back to 1905. The founder died in 1921 and his eldest son, Howard Allison, became president. A younger son was named vice-president, and an old employee, J. C. Nelson, treasurer.

Up to 1926 the concern was very prosperous. At that time its statement showed a net worth of more than $600,000, with yearly sales running above $3,000,000. But then began a gradual decline. Within six years its net worth had shrunk one-fourth, and sales were down to less than $2,000,000. Its inventory turnover was about three times a year, while other wholesale grocers averaged a turnover of five times a year in the same territory.

The concern had done business from the start with one local bank, the Northwestern National, and had been granted from time to time seasonal loans up to $250,000. And so, in view of the fact that the concern was out of the bank's debt at the moment, and in view of the good reputation of the management and the pleasant relations extending over many years, Mr. Rockwell, the bank's president, granted a credit of $200,000 in spite of the unfavorable showing.

Howard Allison attributed the decline of the business to intense competition from grocery chains that were, in those years, spreading rapidly throughout the country. Mr. Allison believed in fighting fire with fire; he had already gone into the chain-store business in a small way; when he secured the $200,000 credit from the Northwestern Bank, he invested a third of the sum in more retail outlets. When the bank president learned of this, he made a vigorous protest, pointing out that money thus invested was in fixed assets that at the best would take years to work out. The banker also doubted if the concern could operate branch stores as successfully as the big, nation-wide chain organizations. He insisted on a complete independent audit so he might know the concern's exact financial position:

ASSETS

Cash	$ 15,293
Accounts receivable	95,581
Inventory	399,682
Current assets	$510,556

Fixed assets	$112,587
Slow receivables	101,336
Other assets	28,700
Total assets	$753,179

LIABILITIES

Notes payable	$153,680
Accounts payable	98,392
Current liabilities	$252,072
Common stock	$300,000
Surplus	137,926
Total liabilities	$689,998
Net working capital	$258,486
Net sales	$934,660
Net profits (loss)	$ 17,326
Dividends	$ 15,000

This statement confirmed the banker's misgivings. Net yearly sales were considerably below sales figures of former years. Accounts payable were nearly three times as great as the average of six years before. The concern's cash on hand was down to an all-time low level.

To the banker, however, the most disturbing item was the amount of fixed assets, nearly three times greater than four years earlier, when the concern began opening its retail stores. The concern could not afford to have so much of its capital tied up in its retail branches. Under the most favorable conditions the branches would take years to produce sufficient revenue to pay back the money invested in them.

Another disturbing factor was the reduced yearly sales volume. To the banker this was an indication that independent retail grocers, on whom the concern had formerly depended for a good share of its business, were resentful of the concern's chain-store activities. They did not care to buy supplies from a concern that carried water on both shoulders—that was in direct competition with them. The increased amount of money tied up in slow receivables seemed proof of this. It indicated that the concern could not sell to prosperous, well rated grocers. It had to be content with selling to grocers who were so poorly financed that they took an unreasonably long time to pay their bills; many, perhaps, would never pay at all.

At the time the Allison Wholesale Grocer Company presented the foregoing balance-sheet, it was operating twenty-one retail stores. It had reduced only fractionally its $200,000 loan at the bank. The bank president informed Howard Allison that, though the bank still had adequate protection for its loan, he was not satisfied with the situation. He pointed out that in spite of a loss on its year's operations the concern had paid $15,000 in dividends, taking the money out of its surplus. He asked Mr. Allison to pay no more dividends until the concern should be on a profitable basis. Mr. Allison agreed to this; but he demurred when the banker suggested that the concern liquidate its retail branches. Mr. Allison still believed a profitable footing might be achieved by continuing the chain-store end, and even increasing the number of retail outlets.

The banker stated that in such case he should be obliged to request liquidation of the concern's bank loan. An agreement was reached by which the concern was to make a monthly payment to the bank of $7,500. But in the course of a year it became apparent that this was beyond the concern's power. During the year there was a sharp increase in fixed assets, and a further reduction in net working capital. Then Howard Allison agreed to liquidate the retail stores and to confine himself to his regular wholesale operations.

Liquidation of the bank loan was accomplished by reduction of the concern's excessive inventory and by cutting down the amount of receivables by a more determined collection policy. At the same time the retail stores were sold, one by one, generally at less than the original investment.

This, of course, caused a steady reduction in the net worth of the concern; yet the money received from the sale of the stores made it possible for Mr. Allison entirely to clear up the bank loan. On a smaller scale the concern attained a healthy financial condition. By closing his retail stores that were a source of irritation to many retail grocers, Mr. Allison was able to get back a considerable number of former customers. At present the concern handles specialty food items exclusively. The Northwestern National Bank grants seasonal loans of moderate amounts, which Mr. Allison is able to retire satisfactorily.

Here, then, is an example of beneficial teamwork between a business man and a banker. It is quite likely that except for the banker's counsel and coöperation the Allison Wholesale Grocery concern would eventually have found itself in the hands of the referee in bankruptcy. The president of the Northwestern National could easily have forced payment of the loan and washed his hands of the concern's affairs. That he did not, we may attribute to the human desire to help a friend in difficulties. But to put it on a very practical basis, with all sympathy left out, the banker, for his own reputation as well as for the reputation of his bank, did not want to have it said that a customer of long and intimate relationship had been permitted to go to the wall.

·CHAPTER XIII·

Credit Crooks

FOR EVERY dollar's worth of cash business transacted in the United States, approximately $100 worth of business is done on credit. Merchandise is shipped in the belief that the recipient will be able to pay the bill when it falls due, and also that he *intends* to pay. Unfortunately there are individuals who scheme to secure merchandise with no intention of paying. It is estimated that losses to manufacturers and wholesalers have averaged more than $250,000,000 during recent years. In many cases these credit crooks display ingenuity worthy of a better cause.

There is a trick that has been worked a great many times, where a crook, or more often a group of crooks, opens a store in some town and gives their enterprise a name that is similar to that of an established, solid firm in the community. If the established firm is, say, A. Smith and Company, the crooks call themselves L. Smith and Co. It helps if the address is also somewhat similar—North Main Avenue, instead of South Main Avenue, the location of the legitimate concern.

It is a situation that calls for more than ordinary vigilance on the part of credit executives. When the crooks begin to order merchandise by mail, it may happen that the executive overlooks the slight change in name or address and allows the order to go through on the assumption that the order came from the same firm that had been buying merchandise in the past and paying satisfactorily.

In the following incident, and others described in this chapter, I have given fictitious names to persons and communities, though the facts are as stated. In a South Carolina town the Palmetto State Mercantile Company was a fine old concern with high credit. The crooks named theirs the "Palmetto State Mercantile and Trading Company," and ordered goods from numbers of manufacturers and wholesalers. In nearly every case the merchandise was shipped without question.

But one credit executive, connected with a Philadelphia manufacturing concern, caught the slightly different name and requested a financial statement before allowing the shipment to go out. He also wired the representative of a credit agency in the South Carolina town to make an investigation. It turned out that the crook establishment was in a recently rented cow-barn at the edge of town, though the stationery used in ordering merchandise gave the impression that the concern had been in business a long time.

At the time of the investigation the cow-barn was practically empty. Merchandise received had been shipped immediately to other towns where the conspirators had connections. A single individual was in charge, the "front man" of the gang. He contended stoutly that the business was legitimate and that the merchandise had been sold to retail customers for cash. He claimed to have sent the money as fast as it came in to a young lady in another state who threatened to expose him as being the father of her child. But he did not know the lady's current address.

The item that finally landed the man in jail was the financial statement he had sent the Philadelphia credit executive, claiming a net worth of some $20,000 in cash, goods, and accounts receivable. Unfortunately for him he had mailed the statement at the local post-office. The credit executive had carefully kept the envelop bearing the post-mark, as proof. The use of the mails in sending erroneous credit information appearing in financial statements comes within the Federal Statute covering the illegal use of the mails.

Some two years ago a wholesale business was started in the Bronx, New York City, whose letter heads bore the title, "Universal Jobbing House, S. Marburg, President." Apparently the concern intended to handle a wide range of commodities. Letters were sent to manufacturers of toys, electrical goods, ladies' ready-to-wear, piece goods, kitchen ware, men's clothing, smokers' articles, and various other lines of merchandise. Each letter requested the manufacturer to send a salesman to the concern's warehouse, and stated that in case the concern gave an order, Mr. Marburg would submit a financial statement as a guarantee of his responsibility.

Salesmen began to call. The concern occupied the second floor of an old side-street building. There was a small lobby at the front to which salesmen were admitted and where the buying was done. Separating this lobby from the main ware-room was a small grating through which it was difficult to see what was going on inside, though dimly could be made out the figures of half a dozen men walking about or sitting at improvised desks.

The letters sent out stipulated that salesmen should ask particularly for Mr. S. Marburg, who was buyer-in-chief. In each case the salesman was treated very courteously and there was little haggling over prices. At the end of the interview the salesman was handed a typewritten statement that listed the Universal Jobbing House's paid-in capital at $12,000, with no liabilities. In no case was the order a large one; only one or two orders were for more than $300, and the majority for less than that sum.

Yet though the orders were not large, they were numerous; within a month more than one hundred manufacturers had delivered merchandise at the Universal Jobbing House address. As bills fell due and no payments were made, collectors who were sent to the address reported the premises to be entirely empty, with not so much as a scrap of paper that might give a clue to the identity of Mr. Marburg or his associates. Even the number on the telephone receiver had been scraped off. Neighboring business men recalled seeing a truck with a New Jersey license-plate carting off goods from day to day, but supposed the concern was merely making deliveries to legitimate customers.

A girl typist was located, but stated she knew nothing about the concern as she had been employed only one week. Her work consisted entirely of typing the financial statements that were handed to salesmen. The identity of Mr. Marburg up to the present time remains a mystery. There were as many "Mr. Marburgs" as there were members of the gang. Whenever a salesman asked to see Mr. Marburg, some person came out who claimed to be that individual. Salesmen who were later called on to describe Mr. Marburg gave widely different descriptions. There was a tall Mr. Marburg, a fat Mr. Marburg, a smooth-shaven Mr. Marburg, a whiskered Mr. Marburg, and a Mr. Marburg who spoke broken English. The total haul of the gang was estimated at about $25,000.

From the best evidence obtainable it is believed that commercial crooks make a profit of a bare third on merchandise, even when they manage to escape detection and subsequent criminal prosecution. If the haul of merchandise amounts to $30,000, the crooks are fortunate to net around $10,000 in cash. Expenses are heavy. A gang must consist of at least four men. There is the "Master Mind," who directs operations; the "front man," who secures the goods; the "mover," who gets the goods away from the immediate community, and the "fence," who maintains a warehouse in some inconspicuous spot where the merchandise is stored until it can be turned into cash. Speed in disposing of the haul is all important; merchandise must be sold at ruinously low prices to tempt quick buyers. And when the members of the gang are apprehended, as they frequently are, lawyers who take their cases demand high fees. More often than not the crooks end up with no profit at all and spend terms in jail beside.

On the second day of November, 1939, two young men called on Mr. Elias Martin, a general store merchant in the small town of Elkhead, Pennsylvania, and stated that they were contemplating the purchase of a prosperous, going retail business. They had been informed that Mr. Martin would not be averse to retirement from active affairs; in case he decided to sell, and would let his business go at a reasonable figure, the young men were prepared to pay spot cash in any amount up to $25,000.

Mr. Martin was impressed with the evident sincerity of the young men and their apparent familiarity with the details of retail trade. They exhibited a caution that was also very reassuring. They would not wish, they informed Mr. Martin, to make a deal of such importance without first learning at first hand just what were the volume of sales, what class of customers patronized the store, and what proportion of the business was done on credit, and what proportion was cash across the counter. They offered Mr. Martin $200 for a two-weeks' option on his business. In case they decided not to buy, the option money was his; if they should buy, the money was to be applied on the purchase price. During the two weeks the young men would spend their time in the store, going over the merchant's books and watching the general trend of the business.

To the merchant the proposal seemed entirely reasonable, and a formal agreement was drawn up. The young men were zealous in attendance at the store. They came early each morning and were admitted by the porter, generally an hour before the arrival of Mr. Martin. They went through the books and learned from what wholesalers and manufacturers he was in the habit of buying merchandise.

At the end of the option period the young men informed Mr. Martin that they were not fully convinced of the wisdom of purchasing the business; they were going away, but might return later. Meanwhile, as per agreement, Mr. Martin could keep the $200 option money.

That seemed to be the end of the affair. But the first of the following month Mr. Martin began to receive statements from manufacturers and wholesalers that showed accounts due in large sums for goods shipped during the time the young men had their option on the business. Mr. Martin had not ordered the goods in question. Investigation revealed what had gone on. All the time the young men were in the store they had been sending mail orders, and in every case requested immediate shipment. Mr. Martin's credit was first class; there was no hesitancy in complying with the request.

The young men, it will be noted, came to the store early in the morning and were on hand when the postman made his delivery. When a letter arrived bearing the imprint of a firm from which goods had been ordered, they opened it, pocketed the invoice and the bill of lading. Later, one of the young men went to the railway freight station, showed the agent the bill of lading and took possession of the shipment. The merchandise never reached Mr. Martin's store. It was quickly loaded on a truck belonging to the young men and carted away to a town in Ohio, where a confederate had rented a store-room.

A good proportion of credit crooks are of foreign extraction, but not many are foreign born. These latter are generally honest. Having had a hard time in the lands of their birth they are likely to appreciate the opportunities that exist here and are willing to work for their money. The trouble starts with the younger generation. They want to get rich without undue labor. With no background of Americanism, or understanding of traditional American ethics, they believe any one is a dull person who will not take short cuts to prosperity; who is satisfied to progress in the old-fashioned way, slowly and honorably.

Almost invariably the commercial crook is a congenital egotist. He looks on money-making as a battle of wits. He is sure he can win over any honest business man. In his make-up there is the desire to make money combined with a still greater desire to prove himself a supremely smart fellow.

There is an old fraud game that has been played many times in the past and that will doubtless be played in the future. It poses a difficult problem for credit men in all lines, wholesaling, manufacturing, and commercial banking. There is a good illustration in a recent case that was worked in a large western city.

A man whom I will call Finlitz purchased an old-established general merchandise concern that did a wholesale and retail business in one of the outlying districts of the city. The owners stood high with their customers and with their merchandise suppliers. Their credit was unquestioned.

The man Finlitz persuaded the owners not to give publicity to the sale of the business. He represented that it might affect sales adversely if regular customers should know of the change in management. Also, unfortunately, the owners agreed to allow him to use the firm's old name until he should become settled in the business. He asked to use the name for three months only, which seemed reasonable enough. But it turned out that three months was sufficient for Finlitz' purpose.

None of the merchandise suppliers was aware of the change in ownership. Immediately Finlitz took charge, he commenced buying. He placed orders with the usual suppliers and with many new ones. The old firm's paying habits were so favorably known that manufacturers and wholesalers had no hesitancy in delivering the goods.

Finlitz put on an aggressive selling campaign to move the merchandise that was coming in from day to day. He had four high-pressure salesmen who called on retail merchants; these men quoted such ridiculously low prices that selling was easy. The only proviso was that retailers should pay spot cash. Merchandise went out of the Finlitz establishment as fast as it came in from suppliers.

A month passed and creditors began to send statements of accounts. Finlitz paid no attention to them. Doubtless some creditors had moments of concern, but no one took action. The credit of the old concern was unassailable.

Another month passed and it became all too evident that something was wrong. Several interested firms applied to the local manager of the National

Association of Credit Men, requesting an investigation. The association man was not long in learning the true state of affairs. Finlitz offered to make an assignment for the benefit of all creditors, but the association man refused the offer. The business was thrown into the bankruptcy court.

Total liabilities were found to be nearly $40,000. Finlitz and his four "salesmen" disappeared. Their last purchase, made from an unsuspecting wholesaler on credit, was for $100 worth of luggage to use on their travels.

Eventually all five were caught. In court Finlitz put up a most ingenious reason for his inability to pay his debts. There had been discovered an account-book that showed daily withdrawals from the business of $300. Finlitz explained that he was an unlucky gambler and each day bet $300 on various horses, invariably losing. The judge was unsympathetic and gave Finlitz two years and six months in the Federal penitentiary for violation of the National Bankruptcy Act.

An enormous commercial racket was unearthed during the nineteen thirties that implicated eleven men, who had secured more than $200,000 worth of merchandise without paying one dollar. It started with a dry-goods store in a Boston suburb. A man opened a business there who called himself A. J.

Morris, though that was only one of the names he adopted later—Marvin, Klemanski, Hazelton, Horowitz. He was an educated man, graduate of a New England college. He opened the suburban store late in August and immediately began to buy merchandise. To the houses from which he made purchases he gave financial statements that showed him to be worth about $10,000; he also named the bank where he had his funds. The bank informed interested inquirers that "Morris" did actually have $10,000 on deposit. The only favor "Morris" asked of suppliers was that they give him three months' dating on his purchases, bills to fall due December first.

The store continued in operation until October first, by which time Morris had accumulated stock worth about $25,000. Then he closed his doors in observance of the Jewish holidays. Goods were left in the show windows; but during the interim the store was cleaned of merchandise, and the proprietor disappeared along with it. Morris was not a person to overlook small profits. On the day preceding the holidays, he hired a man to wash the show windows, whose charge was $3.00. Morris gave him a check for $10, and the man returned $7.00 change. The check was never paid. Morris had drawn his money from the bank that morning.

The $25,000 stock of merchandise was shipped

away to some unknown destination. Morris had that as net profit, earned during his one month operation. And he still had his original $10,000 in cash. Without loss of time he opened business in a South New Jersey town, in a store-room previously rented by a confederate. The name he chose this time was Horowitz.

He went through the same motions as in the Boston suburb, depositing his $10,000 in a local bank to secure a credit rating, then ordering merchandise from manufacturers and wholesalers in widely separate parts of the country. In one instance he secured a sizable shipment of women's garments from a manufacturer in Kansas City. As it was then October, he was able to get January dating on most of his purchases. A few suppliers refused to grant those terms; in such cases he canceled his orders.

Thus Horowitz and his gang had three months in which to make their haul. As soon as an ample stock had been accumulated in the New Jersey store, and the $10,000 had served its purpose, Horowitz drew the money out of the bank and sent it to a confederate who was opening a store in a Pennsylvania town. There the money was, as previously, deposited in a local bank and kept there long enough to establish a credit rating, then sent on to another gang member. By December seven stores were being operated by various members of the gang in

New Jersey, Pennsylvania, and Maryland. All operated at high pressure, offering merchandise at far below market prices. Sales were made for cash only. The greatest haul was made in December; by Christmas, stocks were down to a minimum. Just before January first the racketeers abandoned their stores and disappeared. Some bulky merchandise was left, but everything that could be easily transported was gone, carried in suitcases to rooming-houses in Pittsburgh and New York.

Eventually all eleven gangsters were apprehended and all but two given jail terms on charges of conspiracy and of concealing assets. The "front man" Morris, alias Horowitz, alias Hazelton, etc., was sent to the Federal penitentiary for three years.

Credit crooks turn up in the most unexpected places. Several years ago a young man who gave the unassuming name of Powell called on a number of book-publishing houses in New York to propose a scheme to increase public book buying; he called his scheme the Home Bookshelf. In some respects the plan was similar to the old Tabard Inn Library. The man had very polished manners and the best Boston accent. He had a slight limp and used a cane. He attributed his handicap to the fact that he had been a member of his university's football team and was injured in an intercollegiate game.

Mr. Powell's plan for selling books seemed to have merit if aggressively carried out. It was during the depression of the 1930's with book sales at a low ebb, and publishers were eager to give a trial to anything that promised increased business. Though the man was somewhat hazy when asked for credentials, and frankly stated that he had practically no money, yet his impressive personality inclined several publishers to trust him with stocks of their books and to advance him cash that he stated he needed to start his project. In each case he asked that the books be billed him on open account, but he insisted on giving notes for money advanced. In one case he secured $700 worth of books and $500 in money.

His greatest success was with one of the largest publishing houses in New York, where he secured credit to the amount of $6,000 in books and cash. His approach to the concern was quite clever. He arrived at the concern's offices just before noon. His personality was so impressive that the executive he called on did not feel like putting him off until after lunch. Possibly the man's limp and his cane aroused a bit of sympathy; anyhow, the executive asked his visitor to have luncheon in the concern's private dining-room, maintained for the higher executives.

Whether or not Powell had laid his plans with

the idea of being able to connect with all the executives at the same time, is not known; but anyhow he made the most of the situation. The luncheon was prolonged into a business session and at its end the executives had agreed unanimously to trust Powell with $6,000 in books and cash.

It was estimated that his work among the New York publishers netted something like $20,000. Before any concern began to inquire as to returns from book sales, and before any of the notes Powell had given fell due, he disappeared from the city. He was finally located in Boston; but when legal steps were taken to compel restitution, no assets could be located. None of the publishing firms cared to press criminal charges, and Powell was free to go his way.

Three years passed. Then one of the houses that had been victimized received a telephone call from the small town of Larned, West Virginia, requesting immediate shipment of books to the amount of about $200. The man making the call directed that the books be billed to the Henry Jameson General Store. He said shipment might be made C.O.D., though it would be more agreeable if sixty days' credit were extended. He mentioned a local bank that would testify to the Jameson store's financial responsibility. When the order came to the publisher's credit manager, he decided rather than ship such a large package C.O.D., to get in touch with the bank reference. He wired the bank and received a reply, HENRY JAMESON STORE NOW O.K.

The credit man wasn't entirely satisfied; he recalled the case of the plausible Bostonian who swindled his firm and others on book deals. He decided to let the order go through, but to take immediate action in case the bill was not paid when due. It was not paid; and he engaged a lawyer in the town to force collection. This lawyer reported back that the stock of general merchandise had been seized by wholesale suppliers. He also suggested that the credit man of the publishing house come to Larned. The lawyer had a suspicion that "Henry Jameson" was an assumed name.

It was an extraordinary situation that the credit man encountered. The Henry Jameson General Store had been opened only a short time previously with rather elaborate ceremonies, including a barbecue and music by a brass band. The store was made to resemble an establishment of the old-time horse and buggy era, even to a row of hitching posts in front. Upstairs, in a room above the store, several persons were still engaged in typing letters to be sent to individuals all over the country, strongly condemning President Roosevelt's New Deal. The letters also solicited subscriptions for an organization that Henry Jameson was forming, to enlist boys of sixteen years or thereabouts into a military company. The uniform and other equipment would cost $10 per boy.

It was evident that Jameson was playing up to the prejudices of Fascistically minded persons who bitterly resented the New Deal. In the paragraph of the letters that asked for money he covertly hinted that the military company might be used later on to bring about a political coup. A visit to the bank revealed that Jameson had, up to a few days previously, carried a substantial balance, which explained the bank's telegram, "Henry Jameson Store now O.K." But Jameson had drawn out his money a few days before and left town, saying he was about to go on a trip to buy merchandise for his store. That was the last seen of him. He disappeared completely.

The ingenuity displayed in the West Virginia scheme led the credit manager to suspect that the polished Bostonian "Powell" who had swindled book publishers, and the absconded merchant "Jameson" might be one and the same. In the West Virginia town Jameson did not limp, nor carry a cane. But one slender thread of evidence served eventually to identify Powell and Jameson as the same person. When the man had talked with the credit manager of the swindled publishing house three years earlier he mentioned that he had formerly been in the lumber business on the West Coast and dealt in rare tropical woods from South America. He had made the same statement to the cashier of the Larned bank where he kept his account. Apparently "Jameson" had left town so hurriedly that he was unable to dispose of his store building. It still stood in his name; after certain legal proceedings the publishing house was allowed to dispose of the property and to collect not only its $200 debt, but also to reimburse itself for the merchandise and cash advanced Powell alias Jameson, three years before. It was one of the rare cases where a swindled firm came out even.

· CHAPTER XIV ·

Four Successes

FOR A NUMBER of years past, in my capacity of business writer and investigator, it has fallen to me to visit successful business men in various parts of the country and to write articles analyzing the reasons for their success.

It happens that every man whose career I have analyzed started from scratch. None of them inherited money. With every man it was a case of starting business on money saved from wages. And in each case, as I figured it, the dominant reason for my subject's success lay in the fact that he was not merely a competent business man; he was also a first-class financier.

Their financing took widely different forms.

One man made his success by using his credit to the limit—at one time he went into debt $500,000 when his actual net worth was a mere fraction of that sum. Another man, equally successful, made practically no use of his credit. Throughout his entire career he has operated on a strictly cash basis.

The latter man is Mr. E. S. Ferrill of Buffalo, Kentucky, owner of a wholesale general-merchandise business. Buffalo is a hamlet of fewer than four hundred people, seventy miles south of Louisville. In another chapter I mention Mr. Ferrill as a banker; he operates a bank, of which he is president and principal owner, along with his wholesale mercantile business.

Mr. Ferrill simply happened to get into merchandising. The summer he was twenty years of age he worked, on shares, his father's farm a few miles out from the village of Buffalo. One day that fall he went to the village on some errand and happened to remark to one of the storekeepers that his share of the farm earnings had been $410. The storekeeper, who was not doing well, promptly offered to sell his store, lock, stock, and barrel, for the money young Ferrill had earned.

No capital, outside of that $410, has ever been invested in Mr. Ferrill's business. When he bought the store it was a distinctly one-horse affair with a mixed stock of groceries and drug sundries, badly run down. The former owner had not said how much business the store was doing, but Mr. Ferrill learned, after he became proprietor, that sales were less than $10 a day.

From that beginning Mr. Ferrill has worked sales up to more than $1,250,000 a year. He believes he was able to do this because he stuck to a financial principle. He never added a new line of goods until he had saved up enough money to do it on a cash basis. He never borrowed a dollar to expand on. He made his business earn its own expansions.

He doesn't claim deliberately to have adopted the principle of cash operations. In the beginning it was, simply, that he was afraid of going into debt. Being country raised, he knew what generally happened when a man put a mortgage on his farm. He considered a business debt to be the same as a mortgage and he didn't propose to get into trouble on *that* account. He also determined, as soon as he was able, to keep a little cash on hand for emergencies.

It was really this determination to have a cash reserve that set him on the road to big business. In two or three years he worked his sales up to about $30 a day and had managed to accumulate $300. One day a farmer came in and bought some Epsom salts to doctor a horse. Then he said he wished Mr. Ferrill would handle ordinary salt by the barrel.

"I use a lot of salt for my stock," the farmer said. "Every time I need a barrel I have to drive fifteen miles over to New Haven for it. I'll buy it from you if you can sell it to me at the same price that I pay for it over there."

The farmer's remark changed Mr. Ferrill's whole life. Up to then he never expected to make more than a comfortable living in his cross-roads retail store and perhaps build a home to take the place of the $4-a-month rented house that he and his wife lived in. But the salt business stirred his ambition. If he could get it going it would bring more farmers to his store. His trade in other things would increase.

But there was a catch in it. He couldn't handle salt on a small scale. The farmer said the dealer in New Haven charged $4 a barrel. To make a profit at that price Mr. Ferrill would have to buy in 100 barrel lots, cash in advance. If he did that, he could get it in Louisville for $3 a barrel, and the railroad would grant a carload freight-rate on the haul to the station in New Haven. Buffalo isn't on a railroad line.

Mr. Ferrill thought of his $300 cash reserve, just enough to handle the deal. He had 100 barrels sent down to the New Haven station, then hired men to haul it to Buffalo in two-horse wagons. After paying freight and haulage he could sell his salt to farmers at $4 a barrel and make a reasonable profit.

Mr. Ferrill's salt venture had an unexpected result. There aren't any big towns in his part of Kentucky. Trading is done largely in little hamlets and backwoods settlements. One day a back-road storekeeper drove to Buffalo and said he would buy salt from Mr. Ferrill if Mr. Ferrill would make him a special price so he could sell it to his own farmer-customers at $4 a barrel and make a little on it. "If I order a barrel or two from Louisville," the storekeeper explained, "freight charges more than eat up the profit."

Mr. Ferrill agreed to make the storekeeper a price of $3.60 a barrel, provided he would pay spot cash and cart it away himself. Other back-country storekeepers heard about it and began to come to buy salt. Before long Mr. Ferrill was doing a salt business with merchants from all over the county. He had become a wholesaler almost without knowing it.

Next, when he got some more cash together, he built a frame warehouse back of his store and put in a wholesale stock of fertilizers. He offered storekeepers a special discount as he had done in the salt venture. They could drive their wagons to Buffalo and buy fertilizer cheaper than they could get it from the city and pay small-lot freight rates.

Mr. Ferrill's profits on his wholesale business, plus the profits of his retail store, made it possible for him to add some new line every so often. Eventually he was wholesaling hardware, drugs, stock-feed, farm implements, lumber, groceries. At present he employs a force of traveling salesmen who cover twenty-four Kentucky counties. Twelve big trucks deliver the salesmen's orders. In his seven warehouses Mr. Ferrill carries stocks of practically everything a store-keeper may require. If a store-keeper wants a twenty-gallon wash-boiler for a customer, Mr. Ferrill has it. He also has cow bells, wood stoves, lamp chimneys, calf weaners, horse collars, plow-points, lumber wagons.

Mr. Ferrill doesn't deny that he has made mistakes. Some of the lines he took on proved unprofitable and he had to abandon them. Once he took the agency for a certain make of automobile and put in a stock of cars. But he found it was too complicated a business for a general wholesaler to handle and gave it up, taking his loss. Other ventures cost him money.

Yet in spite of his mistakes, Mr. Ferrill's business went steadily forward to its present huge proportions. His explanation is quite simple. It was sticking to his principle of never taking on a new line until he had the cash to handle it.

"You see," Mr. Ferrill told me, "what that meant.

If I laid down the cash for some new venture, and it turned out poorly, I lost the cash I put into it, but that was all. My regular business wasn't hurt. I could go right ahead as though nothing had happened."

Perhaps the most astonishing thing about the Ferrill business is the way it shot ahead during the long depression of the nineteen thirties. When the débâcle of 1929 occurred, his sales were about $250,000 a year. When the depression perked up, he was doing $1,250,000. To be sure, during that period, Mr. Ferrill had taken his capable son, Jimmy, into partnership. At present Jimmy handles the sales, but his father does the financing.

But it was the financing, I believe, that made possible the astonishing sales jump. The depression wasn't a set-back for E. S. Ferrill and Son. It was an opportunity. When the depression came, Mr. Ferrill wasn't in debt. While other wholesalers were cutting down their inventories and struggling to pay past-due notes, he could buy as freely and discount his bills as he always did. If a manufacturer needed money, Mr. Ferrill could pay for goods in advance. Frequently he did that. He was in shape to take on new customers and go further out for business.

Though Mr. Ferrill is a wealthy man, a bank president, and has a triple-A credit rating in every financial agency in the country, he will not budge an inch from his original policy of refusing to take on a new line of merchandise until he has ready cash to finance it. When I was in Buffalo his son was anxious to add a sash and door department to their lumber business that would cost several thousand dollars. But his father put his foot down. "We haven't enough loose money right now to swing it," Mr. Ferrill said. "We'll have to wait a bit." That ended the discussion. It was simply a reiteration of the financial policy that has worked successfully over the years.

Mr. George M. Davis of Rock Glen, New York, is another business man who has done well in an unlikely place. Rock Glen is fifty miles from Buffalo, and is little more than a wide place in the road, with half a dozen houses. But the Davis general store does a retail business of almost $250,000 a year.

Mr. Davis learned the storekeeping trade in another cross-roads settlement a few miles from Rock Glen. By the time he was in his early twenties he was earning $2.00 a day, which seemed to the boss an extravagant salary; Mr. Davis was let out and a cheaper man put in his place.

But Mr. Davis had saved $1,100. He went to Perry, the biggest village in the county, and opened a grocery store on Main Street. His ambition was to have a general-merchandise store, but if he did that on his small capital there would be just a little sprinkling of one thing and another, not enough of any one thing to satisfy customers.

The merchandising policy that Mr. Davis stuck to all his life is this: Don't spread out too thin. If you've got only enough money to buy a stock of peanuts, don't try to handle anything else. Carry the biggest and best stock of peanuts in town. Be the peanut king. You'll get people coming to you.

Mr. Davis carried only staple groceries in his store. There were half a dozen other grocers in town, all better off than he; they had horses and gaily painted wagons to deliver goods. Mr. Davis couldn't afford a fancy delivery rig, to say nothing of a boy to drive it. He went to the other extreme and bought the plainest delivery rig he could think of. It was a wheelbarrow. Every afternoon he asked his wife to tend the store, while he wheeled groceries around to people's homes. It was good publicity. People were inclined to trade with a young storekeeper who was so earnest about his work.

Oddly, the wheelbarrow gave Mr. Davis a credit rating. The wife of the National Bank president occasionally bought groceries from him and he delivered them in his wheelbarrow. One day when Mr. Davis took his deposit to the bank, the president called him into the back room and asked him how much his sales amounted to and what his expenses were. Finally the president said, "You seem to be an industrious young fellow. Do you think you could do more business if you had a little extra capital?" Mr. Davis thought he could. "All right then," the banker said. "I'll lend you $500 and you can pay it back out of your profits."

Mr. Davis ran his Perry grocery store four years. But then the building he occupied was sold, and the new owner wanted it for his own use. There wasn't another Main Street location to be rented, so Mr. Davis decided to move to Rock Glen, seven miles away. At that time Rock Glen had a salt plant and a big stone quarry, employing nearly two hundred men. There were three general stores. Mr. Davis was well enough off, by then, to carry a full line of groceries and to add a complete stock of men's work shirts and overalls. On his opening day one of the other merchants came to see him and boasted that his sales had amounted to $5,000 that year. Mr. Davis' sales his first year were three times that.

Mr. Davis claimed he did so well because he paid attention to the old adage, "If you haven't got it, you can't sell it." He had just the two lines, groceries and work clothing; but there was scarcely any grocery item that he didn't have in stock, and he could fit any salt-well or quarry workman with a shirt or overalls no matter how big or small the man might be. There wasn't any bank in Rock Glen, so Mr. Davis continued to do business with the banker in Perry. The banker took quite an interest in him and frequently drove over to Rock Glen on a Saturday afternoon. When Mr. Davis planned to add some new line of goods the banker was willing to help him finance it, but he advised Mr. Davis to use his credit with wholesalers as well. "It's always wise," the banker said, "to have good credit in more than one place."

That advice came in handy some years later when the salt works and the stone quarry both went out of business and the workmen moved away with their families, leaving Rock Glen just a country cross-roads. The other storekeepers folded up, but Mr. Davis stayed. For a while he wasn't very prompt in paying his wholesale accounts, but the wholesalers were patient with him, knowing he was doing the best he could. And in time his policy of carrying complete stocks put him on his feet. People found they could get what they wanted at the Davis country store. Now, customers come from fifty miles around. The store even makes sales to people in Buffalo and Rochester.

Mr. Davis never believed in bargain hunting. The store still gets merchandise from the same wholesalers who were patient when Rock Glen lost its industries. The Davis credit is so good that wholesale houses offer any bargains they happen to have without being asked. Some wholesale grocery houses furnish staple goods at a profit of 2 per cent. They know a check will be mailed the same day that the merchandise is delivered at the Davis store.

Thomas J. Blakemore, of Liberal, Kansas, is president of a corporation that operates twenty-six large food markets in towns throughout Kansas, Oklahoma and Texas, with sales of $3,000,000 a year. He also operates a wholesale grocery business, a meat-packing plant, and is president of a National Bank. Mr. Blakemore is the rather rare combination of business executive and financier, one about as strongly marked as the other.

As a lad of seventeen he went from his father's farm in Arkansas to Liberal to work in a grocery store managed by an uncle. The store owner was an old Indian fighter and cattleman named John George, who was also president of a local bank. The store's sales were about $80,000 a year. Its best customers were ranchmen and farmers who came to town in great wagons pulled by six- or eight-mule teams, sometimes from a hundred miles away, and bought supplies to last six months or more.

Young Blakemore clerked in the store until he was twenty-one—when his uncle quit—and Mr. George made him manager at $100 a month. In three more years he had saved up $2,100, and asked Mr. George to sell him the business with that as down payment and the balance on time. Mr. George wouldn't sell, and Tom quit. There was a wholesale house in Wichita that he had been buying goods from, and they gave him a job as traveling salesman. He traveled a year, then went back to Liberal and again asked Mr. George to sell him the store. The manager, during Tom's absence, wasn't a success as a credit man; he had put some thousands of dollars on the books that were uncollectible. This time Mr. George was willing to sell.

Tom Blakemore was twenty-five when he bought the store. Up to that time he had had no experience in owing money. Old Mr. George at the bank paid the merchandise bills. All Tom knew about financing a business was that the important thing was to keep good credit with concerns he bought merchandise from. As every merchant knows, one of the hardest things in the world is to pull large amounts of cash out of a business and at the same time meet current bills and expenses. Tom had to make his payments to John George rain or shine. So he wrote to every wholesaler he dealt with, stating that until he worked off his debt he might need a little extra time on purchases. Every wholesaler promised to coöperate.

Tom paid off his store debt in a little more than three years. By 1927 his sales were running more than $200,000 a year, and he felt strong enough to branch out. He figured that almost any one with ordinary sense and a willingness to work can make a go of a business he can run as a one-man show, but to build an organization and train men to run it successfully takes organizing talent. He opened another store right in Liberal, and ran it on regular chain-store principles as though it were a hundred miles away, instead of just around the corner. He used the basement of the original store as a warehouse; when the manager of the branch needed merchandise he made out an order and the merchandise was delivered to him. The branch did $100,000 the first year. A third store was opened in 1928, in Hooker, Oklahoma, and by 1931 there were seven Blakemore stores.

Good times came to a stop in 1932. That was the beginning of the "dust storm" years, and the Liberal trade territory was the storm center. Winds blew the topsoil off plowed ground, sometimes to the depth of half a foot. Pasture land fared no better. Grass was blown up from the roots; when that didn't happen, the grass was covered with a layer of dust and smothered. During the six years that the dust storms lasted no merchants did a normal business. On an average sales were off fully 60 per cent.

But Mr. Blakemore did an astonishing thing. He kept right on opening new stores in spite of everything. In 1930 the six Blakemore stores did over $1,000,000. Four years later, with fourteen stores, sales were down to $750,000. It was not until 1939 that the Dust Bowl began to pick up.

You might wonder how it was possible to maintain good credit with suppliers, and even to keep on opening new stores, when business was constantly falling off. The secret was, Mr. Blakemore was on extra cordial terms with his creditors. He was never a hand to shop around for casual bargains. He had continued regularly to buy from the same firms that had extended him credit when he first went into business. When he explained that it was only a matter of time when the big national chains would be coming into his territory and he wanted to be big enough to meet their competition, his creditors were willing to back him up. There was quite a bit of credit philosophy in the remark Mr. Blakemore made to me: "The way to have good credit is to show the people you owe money to that it is to their advantage to keep you in business."

Howard D. Johnson of Wollaston, Massachusetts, is head of a chain of roadside restaurants that string along the eastern states from Maine to Florida. The chain grew from a single restaurant to more than two hundred in the space of five years. Mr. Johnson started business with no money and with debts of more than $30,000. He made his success mainly because he had good credit.

Wollaston, where Mr. Johnson grew up, is a Boston suburb. Just across the street from the railway station there was a small newspaper and ice-cream store. Young Johnson was twenty-seven years old when, one morning on his way to take the train for his job in the city, he dropped into the store. The proprietor had just died and a brother-in-law was there trying to sell the place. Young Johnson knew something of the business because as a boy he had carried one of the newspaper routes. The brother-in-law said, "Howard, why don't you buy this business? I'll give you a bargain."

Johnson replied that he didn't have any money, just a few dollars saved from wages. They talked it over several times, and one day the brother-in-law said Johnson could have the business if he would assume the debts. There was $10,000 owing Boston newspaper publishers, another $10,000 owing the brother-in-law, and $8,000 in merchandise obligations. Johnson said he wouldn't dare to go into it without some working capital. The brother-in-law asked if he had $500. Johnson said he believed he could borrow it.

"All right, then," the brother-in-law said. "Borrow your $500 and I'll lend you $2,000 more."

That $2,500 was the first of a long series of borrowings, and also the beginning of young Johnson's long struggle to keep the business afloat. The newspaper routes earned enough to meet rent and other store expenses, but not enough to make a dent in his debts. He planned to build up ice-cream sales, that had run down practically to nothing. Instead of getting his ice-cream from commercial manufacturers, as the former owner had done, he bought a second-hand freezer and hired an expert ice-cream man to come out from Boston evenings to give him lessons. The expert told him the way to build up a trade on ice-cream was to make it richer than the commercial product. He put 22 per cent butter fat in his ice-cream, while most commercial manufacturers were using 12 per cent.

Even during his toughest times Mr. Johnson scraped up enough money to have an accountant go over his books once a month. He sent the accountant's report to all his creditors. He claims that had a good deal to do with keeping him going when he was head over heels in debt.

"If you owe a man money," Mr. Johnson says,

"it's only fair to let him know exactly how your business stands. And when he knows you aren't holding anything back, he isn't going to be hard on you if occasionally you can't pay a bill the day it falls due."

The money Mr. Johnson spent on his monthly check-up turned out to be the best investment he ever made. One day when the accountant finished his job, he remarked, "Howard, you've got a good thing in this home-made ice-cream you're turning out. It's the most profitable part of your business. That's what you want to push."

There was an empty wooden shack at a bathing beach on the outskirts of the town. Johnson rented it for a summer ice-cream stand, paying $500 for the season. When he paid the rent in advance the man said, "Well, young fellow, you've got a lot of imagination, but I've got five hundred dollars!"

But the place did remarkably well. Receipts for the summer amounted to $30,000. More people learned to like Johnson ice-cream. The following summer he opened a larger stand at a Boston resort, and that one did $50,000 in two months.

Still, he was a long way from being able to clean up his debts. About that time a bank in the neighboring town of Quincy put up an office-and-bank building, and fitted up a ground floor room for a restaurant. One day the bank president sent for

Mr. Johnson and proposed that he operate the restaurant. Johnson said he didn't have the capital, he was still in debt at his Wollaston store. The banker offered to loan him what he needed.

It was lucky that by then Johnson had several profitable bathing-beach ice-cream stands, for otherwise the Quincy restaurant might have sunk him. Rent was $10,000 a year and the seating capacity limited. Eventually the bank reduced his rent and gave him more space; but in the first three years his losses totaled $45,000. The main thing he got out of it was a good working knowledge of the restaurant business.

The idea of starting a chain of roadside restaurants came somewhat by accident. A friend had a piece of property on a main traveled highway south of Boston, and suggested to Mr. Johnson that it would be a good location for another Johnson ice-cream stand. He offered to rent it for $600 a year. Mr. Johnson went to look it over and made his friend a counter proposal. "You can make more than $600 a year out of that property," he said. "Go into business for yourself. Put up a nice building for your ice-cream stand and run a high grade restaurant along with it. I'll teach you how to run the restaurant."

The place cost about $15,000. The friend raised half, and Mr. Johnson borrowed enough to make up the balance. The friend signed a contract to handle Howard Johnson ice-cream exclusively. He also agreed to buy other home-made products Mr. Johnson was turning out. That was the same kind of contract that all the later restaurant owners signed. Mr. Johnson actually owns a comparatively small number of Johnson restaurants. The others are bought and paid for by individuals who operate under Howard Johnson rules.

This first roadside restaurant was a success; it gave Mr. Johnson the idea for his chain. He opened four more that year. It happened at the time that a big Boston milk company was negotiating for the purchase of a chain of three suburban restaurants; the price was $145,000. The milk people offered to buy Johnson's restaurants. He didn't want to sell, and made them a proposal. "Why not," he told the milk people, "lend me the money to buy those three restaurants? Do that, and I'll buy from you all the milk and cream that I use in my ice-cream manufacturing. You'll make more money that way than if you were to go into the restaurant business yourselves."

The milk people finally agreed. They loaned him the money to buy the three restaurants, and an additional amount for working capital. The entire loan was $250,000.

Two years later, when there were forty Johnson

restaurants, a Boston brokerage concern asked Mr. Johnson if he would be interested in floating an issue of Howard Johnson Company stock for public subscription. He was tempted; but when he told the milk people about it they offered voluntarily to increase his loan to $500,000 if he would forget about the stock issue and keep his business in his own hands.

I mentioned to Mr. Johnson that it was remarkable how he had always been able to get money when he wanted it. It was still more remarkable that more than half the time loans were offered him without his asking for them.

He didn't consider it remarkable. "There's nothing mysterious about a good credit rating," he said. "All you've got to do is to have a sound plan and to look as though you have the gumption to go through with it."

·CHAPTER XV·

Custodians of Business Health

I WONDER if it sometimes occurs to men who handle the commercial credits of our country that they stand in somewhat the same positions as physicians. They are the custodians of business health.

A first-class credit man, like a first-class physician, believes in preventive measures. He nips dangerous symptoms in the bud. He does not hesitate, when an applicant for credit presents himself, to warn of practices that if followed may lead to serious complications. One warning may go something like this:

"Don't be tempted to overbuy because your credit is good. Bear in mind that when you buy a bill of merchandise, and the merchandise is placed on your shelves, it is not worth what you paid for it. You could not sell it back to the manufacturer or wholesaler at the invoice price. An article of merchandise is not worth what you paid for it until you have found a customer able and willing to buy it. Until then it represents just so much tied-up capital. And if you accumulate too much tied-up capital, there can be only one ending. More failures occur through too much tied-up capital than from almost any other cause."

I assume that many commercial credit men have been impressed, as I have, with the fact that so many eminently successful business men started business on a shoestring—on a capital of $100 or $300 or $500. Was it because at the beginning they were wiser, or worked harder, or because competition was not so keen in the days when they got their starts as in ours?

Nine times out of ten none of those reasons explains the man's success. He is successful because in the beginning he wasn't tempted to go wrong. With his shoestring capital he had no credit rating, so he couldn't overbuy even if he wanted to. He was careful of his money because he had so little of it. If he sold $10 worth of goods one day, he bought $10 worth more. He might have wanted to buy $20 worth, but he couldn't, because no one would trust him for it.

And so, by the time he accumulated enough capital to be a desirable credit risk, he had acquired the habit of caution. When salesmen began to solicit his business with attractive offers of long credit terms on quantity purchases, he took his pencil in hand and figured how much he would save by buying in smaller quantities and earning the 2 per cent, ten days' discount. Anyhow, having gone along so far without owing money, he had a healthy fear of debts. To put it in a sentence; before he was subjected to temptation he had time to learn the fundamentals of business.

There is another point on which a credit man may do a prospective customer a good turn. It quite often happens that a young man who contemplates going into business will ask advice. Shall he go it alone—start from scratch, as the saying is—and trust to make a success by his own efforts? Or shall he buy an established business? The latter course seems to be the better because an established business has a ready-made list of customers who will continue to be customers even though the ownership has changed.

In such a case the credit man's best advice will generally be: Go it alone. Don't buy. To be sure, an established business has customers; but with the best of intentions the seller can not guarantee to deliver the customers to a new proprietor along with the stock and fixtures. And then, no matter how liberally the business has been operated, it is bound to have accumulated some enemies. As every merchant knows, it is much harder to win back a customer who imagines he has been badly treated, than to create a new customer. An enemy generally stays an enemy. An example comes to my mind of a friend, otherwise a reasonable man, who will not go in a certain drug-store where, on an occasion ten years ago, the proprietor was discourteous to him. The place has changed ownership several times, but my friend stays away. To go in, he says, would remind him of that disagreeable incident.

There is still another, and very important, bit of advice that a credit man, as custodian of business health, may give a person who wishes to establish credit: "Remember that the people you owe money to are your friends. Be open and above board with them. If you find yourself in difficulties it is they who will be most likely to help you. They don't want to close you up. It is to their interest to keep you in business. That is the only way they can make money out of you. And it is a good thing to let your creditors see you personally once in a while. Particularly if your business is in a slump and you are behind in your payments. You might write a score of apologetic letters; they would not be nearly so effective as to sit face to face with the man you owe money to and tell him why you got into hot water and what you are sincerely trying to do to get out of it."

Among the problems of credit executives are customers who could pay their bills promptly, but do not. They finance themselves on their suppliers. Recently in conversation a New York manufacturer mentioned a large retail concern in the metropolitan area. "We might do business with them," he said, "but we don't. I could send a salesman there to-morrow and he might come back with an order running into the thousands. But when we put the account on our books we would know it would be six months or a year before we would get our money. The concern is responsible; we could threaten to sue, and we would get a check. But they would never buy from us again. We have no interest in a single sale, so we simply stay away."

There is an acute credit problem that applies particularly to regional wholesale houses. Many manufacturers of nationally popular products sell exclusively to wholesalers, but send out "missionary" salesmen to solicit orders from retailers. When the salesman secures an order, it is relayed to some wholesale concern that the retailer designates. The wholesaler ships the goods and carries the account.

It is precisely at the moment when the salesman asks the merchant which wholesale house he wishes to have the goods come through, that the credit efficiency of the various wholesale houses is tested. There is a curious twist of human nature that makes a man hesitate to add to a debt already large. The storekeeper runs through his mind the amounts he owes different houses. He may be perfectly solvent, and so good a credit risk that any wholesaler would be glad to handle the business. But almost invariably the house to which he is least in debt gets the merchant's order.

It is a delicate matter, that of steering between too much strictness and too much liberality in credits—of knowing when to be lenient toward a conscientous debtor who is temporarily not in a position to pay his bills on the due date; when to be firm with a debtor who is slow because he may be milking his business of cash for outside investment, or spending too much money on personal living, or because he is simply careless of his obligations. There is an old saying among retail merchants: "When your customers are paid up, they buy from you. When they owe you, they go to your competitor." The saying applies just as strongly to wholesale concerns that accept orders sent in by "missionary" salesmen. If the concern has a too easy-going credit policy it doesn't get the business.

I believe it is legitimate criticism to say that ordinarily there is too little system in the manner in which commercial credits are handled. In a rather wide acquaintance among merchants I do not know of one whose credit relations with his suppliers are conducted on as businesslike a basis as his credit relations with his bankers.

When a merchant goes to his bank for accommodation there is a definite understanding as to the amount he may borrow. A "line of credit" is established. The merchant's borrowings may go to $1,000, $10,000 or $100,000 as the case may be. Knowing what his limit is, the merchant has a wholesome feeling of responsibility in the matter. Consciously or unconsciously he plans his affairs with that debt limit in mind. He watches his step.

But all too often there is not the same feeling of responsibility in the merchant's dealings with his manufacturers or wholesalers. Because there is no definite "line of credit," he is tempted to place orders more lavishly than his capital warrants. Eventually he may find himself unable to meet his obligations.

When a commercial bankruptcy occurs, what, generally, are the losses? Let us suppose a merchant fails and his store is closed by the sheriff. There is in the store a stock that cost $10,000. The debts amount to the same sum. Theoretically, of course, the creditors would get a hundred cents on the dollar for their claims, less a small percentage to cover the expense of administering the business. To an outsider it would seem the creditors should get at least $.75 on the dollar. Experienced credit men know that is an all too optimistic surmise. If the stock nets creditors $.40 on the dollar it is an unusually happy event. More likely the net is $.20, or $.10, or nothing at all.

The moment a business house closes its doors a tremendous slump takes place. Merchandise deteriorates, becomes damaged, goes out of style; court costs and other expenses run up. And the merchandise creditors are not the only losers. The entire community loses. The bankrupt merchant lives on relatives, perhaps, until he finds something else to do. His clerks also join the ranks of the unemployed. The landlord of the building has an empty store on his hands that he can scarcely hope to rent at its former figure because a store that has housed a failure has a bad name. And, moreover, an empty store is a detriment to neighboring merchants; it gives an air of stagnation to the location.

Recently, in conversation with the president of a nationwide financial corporation at its New York headquarters, I spoke of the number of gray-haired executives who seemed to occupy key positions. The president explained that his company's policy was not a gesture of charity toward long-term employees; any man could retire on a pension after a certain number of years' service. "We try to keep some old-time executives with us," the president said, "as a form of insurance. A young fellow coming up in the organization is inclined to believe in short-cuts. Our older men are here to tell the young fellows not only that short-cuts don't usually work, but that most short-cuts have been tried out before."

I have read, in a business journal of considerable standing, an astonishing suggestion for a short-cut to country-wide prosperity. It was an article bearing the title, "Why Not Abolish All Credit Departments?" The author contended that prosperity is held back by credit restrictions. If the credit lid were taken off, if credit were granted to all comers, sales of merchandise would enormously be increased and prosperity would automatically follow. It was admitted there would be losses; conceivably there would be an added number of bankruptcies; but such setbacks would amount to little in view of vastly increased business activity.

My own reaction to the article was one of amazement that it should have appeared in a responsible journal. I have no knowledge of the author, though it may be assumed he is quite young. All our economic crashes—1837, 1857, 1873, and up to 1929—were brought about by precisely the short-cut proposed, that of taking off the credit lid.

It may be said that the best safeguard against

wild short-cut proposals is the conscientious, day-by-day work of the thirty-odd thousand American credit men. They are the custodians of business health.

Index

(1)

2 5 5

CPSIA information can be obtained
at www.ICGtesting.com
Printed in the USA
LVHW081516180422
716530LV00009B/394

9 781014 114365